WITHDRAWN

356-1
58

Supplemental Security Income

The New Federal Program for the Aged, Blind, and Disabled

Paul L. Grimaldi

American Enterprise Institute for Public Policy Research
Washington, D.C.

Paul L. Grimaldi is associate professor of economics at the W. Paul Stillman School of Business, Seton Hall University, South Orange, New Jersey.

Library of Congress Cataloging in Publication Data

Grimaldi, Paul L
  Supplemental security income.

  (Studies in social security and retirement policy)
  (AEI studies ; 253)
  1. Supplemental security income program—United
States. I. Title. II. Series. III. Series: Ameri-
can Enterprise Institute for Public Policy Research.
AEI studies ; 253.
HD7125.G74   362.4'0973   79-25978
ISBN 0-8447-3356-3

AEI Studies 253

Printed in the United States of America

CONTENTS

LIST OF TABLES

LIST OF FIGURES

INTRODUCTION

The Supplemental Security Income (SSI) program represents a landmark effort by the federal government to revamp its welfare programs for the aged, blind, and disabled. SSI was enacted in October 1972 as part of the 1972 amendments to the Social Security Act and became effective on January 1, 1974.[1] One of its major purposes was to provide more equitable welfare payments by replacing the myriad state-operated programs with a uniform nationwide program administered by the Social Security Administration. Another purpose was to provide the states with fiscal relief from mushrooming welfare costs.

Chapter 1 explains the principal features of the SSI program and compares SSI with welfare programs existing before 1974. Chapter 2 presents statistical information on the effect of SSI on the number of welfare recipients and the amount of financial assistance received. Chapter 3 analyzes the success of SSI in raising household income above the poverty threshold. Chapter 4 compares state welfare payments before and after the advent of SSI and examines the impact of SSI on the amount of federal welfare dollars received by the states. Chapter 5 reviews certain aspects of the administrative efficiency of SSI. Chapter 6 discusses the relationship between SSI and the social security system's Old Age, Survivors, Disability, and Health Insurance program (OASDHI). Chapter 7 considers the possible impact of some current welfare reform proposals on SSI.

Joan Curran provided research assistance in the preparation of this study.

---

[1] Public Law 92-603.

1

The SSI Program

The Supplemental Security Income program provides the first, and only, nationally guaranteed minimum level of income to a particular segment of the population—the aged, blind, and disabled. This chapter discusses the major features of the program. The discussion is not intended to be comprehensive, but rather to highlight the most important aspects of the program and to compare SSI with the programs it replaced.

Payment Standards

The monthly SSI payment standards from 1974 to 1979 for the basic needs of individuals and couples living independently are shown in Table 1. These standards are the maximum amount paid for food, clothing, shelter, and other essentials of daily living to persons who have no countable income and satisfy all other eligibility criteria. In addition to the allowance for basic needs, additional payments may be made to cover special needs arising from emergencies and other extraordinary circumstances.

Before SSI, aged, blind, and disabled persons could receive welfare payments under one of the following programs: Old Age Assistance, Assistance to the Blind, Assistance to the Permanently and Totally Disabled, and Assistance to the Aged, Blind, and Disabled.[1] Payment standards, as well as other eligibility prerequisites, were established by the states, subject to federal regulations and guidelines. Payments to persons with no countable income often equaled the

---

[1] For a description of individual state programs, see U.S. Department of Health, Education, and Welfare, *Characteristics of State Public Assistance Plans under the Social Security Act*, Report no. 50 (1974).

TABLE 1

FEDERAL SSI PAYMENT STANDARDS, 1974–1979
(dollars)

Effective Date	Monthly Payment	
	Individuals	Couples
January 1, 1974[a]	130.00	195.00
January 1, 1974	140.00	210.00
July 1, 1974	146.00	219.00
July 1, 1975	157.70	236.60
July 1, 1976	167.80	251.70
July 1, 1977	177.80	266.70
July 1, 1978	189.40	284.10
July 1, 1979	208.20	312.30

NOTE: These standards are for the basic needs of persons living independently and having no countable income.

[a] Original legislation.

SOURCE: Social Security Administration, *Supplemental Security Income for the Aged, Blind, and Disabled: Summary of State Payment Levels, State Supplementation, and Medicaid Decisions,* various issues.

state standard but, because of fiscal constraints or the lack of political support for income transfers, were sometimes less than the state standard.[2] In general, payment standards differed considerably between states and even within the same state. Intrastate variations were usually attributed to area differences in housing costs.

Federal Payment Standards. SSI established uniform federal payment standards. Initially, every eligible person living independently and having no countable income was guaranteed a monthly federal payment of $130. Eligible couples were guaranteed an additional 50 percent, or a payment of $195. In many states, these SSI payment levels were higher than those in effect on July 1, 1973. As Table 2 shows, twenty states had a standard of less than $130 for aged individuals, and sixteen states previously had a standard of less than $195 for elderly couples.

---

[2] For example, in July 1973, Mississippi paid 46 percent of its full standard ($162), or the amount that the state recognized as necessary for basic needs, to aged persons who lived independently and had no countable income. Similarly, fifteen other states paid less than the full standard to such persons. See U.S. Department of Health, Education, and Welfare, *Public Assistance Programs: Standards for Basic Needs, July 1973* (March 14, 1974), table 1.

By January 1, 1974, the federal SSI standards had been raised to $140 for individuals and $210 for couples. The standards have been increased several times since then because of automatic, legally mandated, cost-of-living adjustments. In addition, on July 1, 1975, the Congress awarded all SSI recipients an extra, one-time $50 payment. In July 1979 the standards reached $208 for individuals and $312 for couples.

State Supplementary Standards. In addition to federal SSI payments, eligible persons may also receive state supplementary SSI payments. These payments may be mandatory or optional. Mandatory payments must be made to "grandfathered"—that is, transferred or converted—recipients. Although these payments were not part of the original legislation, they were enacted shortly before SSI was implemented because the Congress believed that some recipients residing in states where previous payments exceeded SSI standards might be hurt financially by the new program.[3] According to this legislation, a state that failed to make mandatory payments could lose matching federal funds for its Medicaid program. In January 1977 about 8 percent of the SSI recipients in twenty-seven states (123,000 persons) received mandatory supplementary payments; three-fourths of them resided in California, Massachusetts, and New York.[4]

Optional supplementary payments are made at the discretion of the state, with the state establishing the amounts and designating the people receiving them. A state can, however, vary its optional payments for cost-of-living differences attributable to three geographical areas of residence and five living arrangements. The states determine both the areas and the arrangements; the latter can include recipients living alone, with an ineligible spouse or relative, in a nursing home, in a residential care facility, or in any other arrangement defined by the state.

Optional payments may cover both basic and special needs. The most popular payments for special needs enable recipients to cover home maintenance costs—for items such as essential furniture and equipment, utilities, property taxes, and garbage collection. Other special needs relate to a recipient's health status, including allowances for guide dogs and therapeutic diets. Twenty-six states and the District of Columbia made optional supplementary payments for special

---

[3] Public Law 93-66, July 1973.

[4] U.S. Congress, Senate, Committee on Finance, *The Supplemental Security Income Program*, 95th Congress, 1st session, April 1977, p. 77.

TABLE 2

Public Assistance and Combined Federal and State SSI Payment Standards for Aged, Blind, and Disabled Recipients Living Independently and Having No Countable Income, 1973, 1974, and 1978

(dollars)

Region/State	Aged Units						Disabled Individuals			Blind Individuals		
	Individuals			Couples								
	1973	1974	1978	1973	1974	1978	1973	1974	1978	1973	1974	1978
United States	—a	140	189	—a	210	284	—a	140	189	—a	140	189
Region I												
Connecticut	181	238	296	229	286	497	181	238	296	181	238	296
Maine	130	140	199	260	260	299	130	140	199	130	140	199
Massachusetts	204	223	316	302	316	481	188	215	304	180	242	343
New Hampshire	173	173	216	228	228	302	173	173	216	173	173	216
Rhode Island	195	171	223	262	267	347	195	171	223	195	171	223
Vermont^b	196	204	226	252	259	352	196	204	226	196	204	226
Region II												
New Jersey	162	182	207	222	250	293	162	182	207	162	182	207
New York	168	207	250	241	295	360	168	207	250	168	207	250
Region III												
Delaware	170	150	189	248	248	284	150	140	189	228	150	189
District of Columbia	128	140	189	160	210	284	128	140	189	128	140	189
Maryland	96	140	189	131	210	284	96	140	189	96	140	189
Pennsylvania	146	150	222	218	230	333	146	150	222	115	150	222
Virginia	152	152	189	196	210	284	152	152	189	123	152	189
West Virginia	123	140	189	180	210	284	123	140	189	123	140	189

Region IV												
Alabama	115	140	189	230	230	302	95	140	189	125	140	189
Florida	132	140	189	181	210	284	132	140	189	132	140	189
Georgia	99	140	189	167	210	284	99	140	189	99	140	189
Kentucky	111	140	189	190	210	284	111	140	189	111	140	189
Mississippi	75	140	189	150	210	284	75	140	189	75	140	189
North Carolina	112	140	189	153	210	284	112	140	189	120	140	189
South Carolina	90	140	189	141	210	284	90	140	189	110	140	189
Tennessee	97	140	189	172	210	284	97	140	189	97	140	189
Region V												
Illinois	171	175	185[c]	215	218	267[c]	171	175	185[c]	171	175	185[c]
Indiana	100	140	189	200	210	284	80	140	189	125	144	189
Michigan	184	160	217[c]	230	240	325	184	160	217	184	160	217
Minnesota	183	178	211	245	258	311[c]	183	178	211[c]	183	178	211[c]
Ohio	131	140	189	222	218	284	121	140	189	131	140	189
Wisconsin	201	216	276	245	329	423	201	216	276	201	216	276
Region VI												
Arkansas	120	140	189	220	220	284	120	140	189	120	140	189
Louisiana	107	140	189	202	210	284	70	140	189	105	140	189
New Mexico	116	140	189	155	210	284	116	140	189	116	140	189
Oklahoma	134	155	231	220	240	363	134	155	231	134	155	231
Texas	123	140	189	200	210	284	123	140	189	123	140	189
Region VII												
Iowa	127	140	189	194	210	284	127	140	189	148	158	211
Kansas	203	203	225	247	242	284	203	203	225	203	203	225
Missouri	85	140	189	170	210	284	80	140	189	100	140	189
Nebraska[b]	197	207	278	265	280	378	197	207	278	197	207	278
Region VIII												
Arizona	130	140	189	180	210	284	130	140	189	130	140	189
Colorado	149	165	229	298	330	458	123	155	206	121	155	206
Montana	115	140	189	193	210	284	115	140	189	115	140	189

TABLE 2—Continued

| | Aged Units | | | | | | Disabled Individuals | | | Blind Individuals | | |
| | Individuals | | | Couples | | | | | | | | |
Region/State	1973	1974	1978	1973	1974	1978	1973	1974	1978	1973	1974	1978
North Dakota	125	140	189	190	210	284	125	140	189	125	140	189
South Dakota	190	190	212	230	230	299	190	190	212	190	190	212
Utah	121	140	199	162	210	294	121	140	199	131	140	199
Wyoming	120	140	209	200	210	324	120	140	209	120	140	209
Region IX												
California	200	235	322	364	440	602	193	235	322	215	265	363
Hawaii	136	165	205	207	248	308	136	165	205	136	165	205
Nevada	175	185	229	279	298	361	—d	185	189	155	215	292
Region X												
Alaska	250	250	377	350	350	553	250	250	377	250	250	377
Idaho	182	192	243	219	234	344	182	192	243	182	192	243
Oregon	153	163	201	221	236	294	153	163	189	166	183	226
Washington[b]	159	170	230	227	243	329	159	170	230	159	170	230

NOTE: Numbers are rounded to nearest dollar. Data for 1973 and 1978 are as of July 1; for 1974, as of January 1. SSI standards are for transferred recipients. Standards may be lower for persons newly eligible after 1973. The standards for 1973 equal the largest amount paid, which may be less than the full standard.

a No national standard.

b SSI standard in certain areas of the state.

c Standard on July 1, 1977.

d No program.

SOURCES: U.S. Department of Health, Education, and Welfare, *Public Assistance Programs: Standards for Basic Needs, July 1973* (March 14, 1974), tables 1–4; Social Security Administration, *Supplemental Security Income for the Aged, Blind, and Disabled: Summary of State Payment Levels, State Supplementation, and Medicaid Decisions* (May 3, 1974, and October 1, 1978); and unpublished data provided by the Social Security Administration.

needs in January 1975.[5] More than half these states made payments for no more than three special needs, but California, Connecticut, and Oregon covered at least seven of these needs.

Combined Federal and State Standards for Basic Needs. The state standards existing on July 1, 1973, and the combined federal SSI and state supplementary standards for January 1, 1974, and July 1, 1978, are shown by state in Table 2.[6] The data are arranged by federal region to highlight the geographic impact of the SSI program. The 1974 and 1978 state supplements can be calculated by subtracting the federal standard from the amounts shown in those years.

A comparison of the July 1973 standards and those of January 1974 shows that SSI substantially increased the welfare income of many aged, blind, and disabled persons. Southern states tended to register the largest relative increases, primarily because their previous standards were low. The monthly standard for an aged person in Mississippi, for instance, rose by 87 percent, as compared with a rise of 18 percent in California and 12 percent in New Jersey. Similarly, many disabled persons in Alabama received 47 percent more in monthly assistance income, as compared with an increase of 23 percent in New York and 2 percent in Illinois.

In July 1978, many states paid optional supplements for the basic needs of at least some SSI recipients. As Table 2 suggests, there were large differences among the states in the scope and magnitude of the optional payments for single persons residing independently in the community. In eight states, monthly optional payments to single aged persons were at least $50; in twenty-four states, they were more than $10. Optional payments to couples were larger in each state, although the states do not always pay couples 50 percent more than single persons, as is done at the federal level. Colorado, for instance, paid twice as much to couples as single persons, whereas New Jersey paid a larger supplement to individuals. Optional payments to elderly couples in California and Massachusetts were much larger than those in the rest of the nation. Couples in California received a supplement

---

[5] For more details, see Social Security Administration, "State Supplementary Payment Provisions under SSI, January 1975," *Research and Statistics Note*, note 2 (March 1977), chart A.

[6] The 1974 figures for many states do not reflect the first set of supplements. In 1973, each state had submitted to the Social Security Administration its standards based on the enabling legislation. The pre-1974 standards can be found in Social Security Administration, *Supplemental Security Income Program for the Aged, Blind, and Disabled: Summary of State Payment Levels, State Supplementation and Medicaid Decisions* (December 18, 1973).

of $318 and those in Massachusetts got $197, as compared with less than $75 in most other states.

Allowances for Essential Persons. Numerous states have historically had allowances for "essential" persons, usually an ineligible spouse or a relative who resides with or cares for a welfare recipient. The 1972 amendments to the Social Security Act prohibit federal payments for such allowances. The law does, however, permit additional federal payments to SSI recipients whose December 1973 payments included an allowance for an essential person according to the state plan in effect in June 1973. The maximum federal payment for essential persons in July 1979 was about $104—the difference between the standards for an individual and a couple. The income and resources of an essential person, as well as those of the recipient, are considered in calculating SSI payments. Payments for an essential person are made as long as this person resides with an eligible person or until the essential person becomes eligible for SSI either in his or her own right or as an eligible spouse of an SSI recipient. The number of essential persons has declined steadily since SSI began, from about 105,000 people in 1974 to 36,000 in 1977.[7]

Institutionalized Persons. Payment standards and eligibility criteria for institutionalized persons vary by type of institution. Residents of medical institutions may receive SSI payments under certain conditions. According to the law, reduced SSI payments are made "in any case where an eligible individual or his eligible spouse (if any) is, throughout any month, in a hospital, extended care facility, nursing home, or intermediate care facility receiving payments (with respect to such individual or spouse) under a state plan approved under title XIX (Medicaid)."[8] The maximum federal payment is $25 a month, but state supplements may raise the amount to higher levels.

The Social Security Administration reduces payments for persons if Medicaid pays more than half the cost of their care. The usual reason for the reduction is that a patient living in a medical facility needs less income than someone in the community because Medicaid is paying the bulk of ordinary living expenses. If Medicaid pays less than 50 percent, a patient may be entitled to the full federal payment regardless of whether Medicare, private insurance, or the patient pays the portion of the cost not reimbursed by Medicaid. In June

---

[7] Lenna D. Kennedy, "Ineligible Spouses of SSI Beneficiaries, December 1976," *Social Security Bulletin*, vol. 41 (August 1978), p. 19.

[8] Public Law 92-603, section 1611(e)(B).

1977 more than 200,000 persons in Medicaid institutions—ranging from less than 2 percent of all SSI recipients in three states to 17.3 percent in Minnesota—received an SSI payment.[9]

SSI payments are made to residents of domiciliary care facilities or boarding homes, or to persons residing under similar supervised living arrangements.[10] Unlike skilled nursing and intermediate care facilities, these facilities do not provide ongoing medical care. Instead, they provide the residents with general supervision, room and board, personal care, and other services. Medicaid reimbursement is not available for the nonmedical services the residents receive, but frequently it can be obtained for their medical care.

Residents of public domiciliary care or other public residential homes are ineligible for standard federal SSI payments if the facility has more than sixteen beds. If it has sixteen or fewer beds or if it is privately owned, the residents may qualify for the standard SSI payment. Further, the states can elect to supplement the federal payment. Many states have special provisions for those receiving domiciliary care; some vary the supplement by type of facility because of cost differentials in meeting resident needs; others pay more for persons in licensed than unlicensed facilities. In fifteen states for which data are available, more than 106,000 SSI recipients resided under supervised living arrangements in March 1976. Table 3 shows the payment standards for residential facilities in selected states effective July 1, 1978.

SSI may encourage states to discharge patients indiscriminately from mental hospitals and nursing facilities to domiciliary facilities in order to save money.[11] Savings are possible insofar as the decrease in the state's share of Medicaid payments for institutional care exceeds its share of the increase in the cost of providing services in alternative living arrangements. In general, the savings can be substantial

---

[9] Social Security Administration, "SSI Recipients in Medicaid Institutions, June 1977," *Research and Statistics Note*, note 14 (December 8, 1978), table 2.

[10] Social Security Administration, *SSI Recipients in Domiciliary Care Facilities: States with Federally Administered Optional Supplementation, March 1976* (1978); and "Domiciliary Care Facilities under the SSI Program in Selected States," *Research and Statistics Note*, note 1 (February 20, 1976).

[11] Congressman Claude Pepper (Democrat, Florida), chairman of the House Select Committee on Aging, recently released the results of a committee survey showing that many patients are being "discharged wholesale," frequently to "slum housing" with little follow-up and after-care services. The major reason given for the discharges is to save money for the states. See the committee press release dated May 26, 1978. Also, see U.S. Congress, Senate, Subcommittee on Long-Term Care of the Special Committee on Aging, *Nursing Home Care in the United States: Failure in Public Policy, Introductory Report*, 93rd Congress, 2nd session, December 1974, pts. 2 and 3.

TABLE 3

Combined Federal and State SSI Payment Standards for Domiciliary Facilities and Other Supervised Living Arrangements in Selected States, July 1, 1978
(dollars)

State/Type of Facility	Individuals	Couples
California		
Nonmedical board and care	396.00	738.00
Delaware		
Certified adult residential home	276.60	542.30
Florida		
Adult foster care home	230.00	460.00
Kentucky		
Personal care facility	350.00	700.00
Massachusetts		
Licensed rest home	350.21	700.42
Michigan		
Personal care	389.33	778.66
New Jersey		
Licensed sheltered boarding home	315.00	630.00
New York		
Congregate care I		
Area A	313.30	626.60
Areas B and C	275.30	550.60
Congregate care II	444.20	888.40
Wisconsin		
Nonmedical group home	310.00	620.00

SOURCE: Social Security Administration, *Supplemental Security Income for the Aged, Blind, and Disabled: Summary of State Payment Levels, State Supplementation, and Medicaid Decisions* (October 1, 1978).

because the greater availability of SSI payments to those receiving domiciliary care enables them to finance a larger amount of their living expenses, which are less expensive than those provided in medical facilities.

Cost-of-Living Adjustments

Federal SSI payments are automatically adjusted annually for increases in the cost of living. This differs noticeably from procedures under former programs in which cost-of-living adjustments depended upon approval by individual state legislatures. Under SSI, adjustments are automatically triggered whenever the consumer price index (CPI) increases by more than 3 percent a year. The purpose of these adjust-ments is to maintain the purchasing power of SSI payments and, to a lesser extent, a recipient's aggregate income. However, three factors limit their effectiveness.

First, states were not required to "pass along" cost-of-living increases to SSI recipients before October 1976. A state could have used increases in federal standards as an opportunity to reduce its outlays for supplementary payments. As a result, the combined federal-state standards would have remained the same or increased by less than the cost-of-living increase in federal standards. A state might have done this in order to reduce its outlays for welfare programs.

Second, using the CPI to adjust federal standards does not make any adjustment for regional variations in inflation. For example, while the national CPI (1967=100) reached 199.1 in September 1978, the CPI for Chicago, Illinois–Northwestern Indiana was 193.0 and it was 205.4 for San Diego, California. Furthermore, inflation need not have the same impact on all income groups. The national increase may understate the effect of inflation on poor persons if the poor spend relatively more of their income on commodities experiencing large price increases.[12] On the other hand, the national increase may over-state the impact of inflation if the poor receive in-kind transfers, such as Medicaid, food stamps, and public housing.[13]

Third, the timing of the cost-of-living adjustment does not always coincide with the timing of the price increase. Because SSI standards are raised in July to compensate for price increases that occurred between the first quarter of the present and past years, the adjustment

---

[12] Hollister and Palmer have constructed a "poor person's price index" (PPI) based on average spending patterns of households having incomes at the official poverty threshold. Their results suggest that between 1960 and 1972 the impact of inflation on the poor was similar to the impact on other households. Between early 1973 and mid-1974, prices increased faster for the poor: the PPI was up 19.4 percent, as compared with an increase of 17.4 percent for the consumer price index (CPI). This difference was attributable largely to rising prices for food and utilities, which make up a larger proportion of the budgets of low-income persons. See Robinson G. Hollister and John L. Palmer, "The Impact of Inflation on the Poor," in Kenneth E. Boulding and Martin Pfaff, eds., *Redistribution to the Poor: The Grants Economics of Income Distribution* (Belmont, Calif.: Wadsworth Publishing Co., 1972), pp. 240–69.

[13] Special "crude" price indexes prepared by the Department of Health, Education, and Welfare suggest that between 1971 and 1975 price increases for goods and services consumed by the poor outstripped price increases to the nation by about 4 percentage points. See U.S. Department of Health, Education, and Welfare, *The Measure of Poverty: A Report to Congress as Mandated by the Education Amend-ments of 1974* (April 1976), p. 93.

11

lags the price increase by several months. This could result in financial hardships for SSI recipients when prices increase substantially.

Attempts to adjust payment levels for interregional variations in inflation rates would be expensive and might encounter empirical and, perhaps, political problems. A major difficulty would be establishment of the areas for which alternative price indexes would be constructed. Regional and state-wide boundaries would pose fewer problems than smaller jurisdictions, but they would not adjust for intrastate differences in cost-of-living increases. In addition, the smaller the number of areas with separate price indexes, the greater the possibility of complaints about unfair treatment.

The loss in purchasing power caused by the time lag cannot be completely remedied unless the government takes the unlikely step of increasing payment levels in anticipation of inflation. Nevertheless, a portion of the financial hardship of the lag could be eliminated if the payment standards were price adjusted every six months instead of annually.

Between January 1, 1974, and July 1, 1977, the federal SSI standard for individuals increased by $37.80; the standard for couples, by $56.70. In general, recipients in states that did not make supplementary payments were automatically eligible for the full inflation adjustment because these states had no choice but to pass them along. Before October 1976, SSI recipients in the remaining states may not have benefited fully, if at all, from specific adjustments. Since then, however, federal law has required the states to pass along to SSI recipients the cost-of-living adjustments in federal standards.[14]

The states have reacted differently to the cost-of-living adjustments both for the interval as a whole and at different points in time. Many states did not pass along all of the July 1974 increase because the January 1974 standards were above the 1973 standards and a pass-along was at state expense. Virtually every state did, however, pass along at least part of the subsequent increases. Some elected to pass along relatively more of the increase to individuals than couples; others did the opposite. A few states favored newly awarded recipients over grandfathered recipients. Several states even raised their standards above the federal increase.

Table 4 shows the dollar changes in the combined federal-state standards for the basic needs of aged grandfathered recipients from January 1, 1974, to July 1, 1977. The changes are shown only for the states in which the combined standard exceeded the federal level on

---

[14] See Chapter 4, fn. 14.

TABLE 4

Dollar Change in the Combined Federal SSI and State
Supplementary Standards for the Basic Needs of Aged Recipients,
by Amount and State, January 1, 1974–July 1, 1977

Dollar Change	State
Individuals	
$1 to $15	Illinois, Kansas, New Hampshire, South Dakota, and Vermont
$16 to $30	Connecticut, Delaware, Hawaii, New Jersey, Oregon, and Virginia
$31 to $40	Idaho, Minnesota, Nevada, New York, Rhode Island, and Wisconsin
$41 to $50	Colorado, Michigan, and Washington
$51 to $65	California, Nebraska, Oklahoma, and Pennsylvania
Over $65	Alaska and Massachusetts
Couples	
$1 to $20	Delaware
$21 to $40	Kansas, Maine, New Hampshire, New Jersey, and South Dakota
$41 to $55	Arkansas, Connecticut, Hawaii, Illinois, Minnesota, Nevada, New York, Ohio, and Oregon
$56 to $75	Alabama, Idaho, Michigan, Rhode Island, Vermont, Washington, and Wisconsin
$76 to $100	Colorado, Nebraska, Oklahoma, and Pennsylvania
Over $100	Alaska, California, and Massachusetts

Note: Recipients living independently, having no countable income, and receiving welfare payments on December 31, 1973. Changes for states with supplementary standards on January 1, 1974.

Sources: U.S. Department of Health, Education, and Welfare, *Public Assistance Programs: Standards for Basic Needs, July 1973* (March 14, 1974); and Social Security Administration, *Supplemental Security Income for the Aged, Blind, and Disabled: Summary of State Payment Levels, State Supplementation, and Medicaid Decisions* (October 1, 1978).

January 1, 1974. Many of these states did not pass along the full federal increase of $37.80 for individuals and $56.70 for couples. Illinois and New Hampshire, for example, passed along less than $15 for aged individuals, whereas six states passed along less than $40 for aged couples. At the other end of the spectrum, several states passed along more than the federal increases. In Massachusetts and California the supplementary increases for couples were twice the federal increase.

13

Income Disregards

Persons who have income from other sources receive smaller SSI payments than persons with no countable income. Certain types and amounts of income can, however, be ignored in determining the payment. The exclusions are called "income disregards," and the amount of income applied against the payment standard is referred to as countable income. Countable income includes unearned, earned, and in-kind income.[15] The larger the amount of income disregarded, the larger the nonwelfare income an individual can receive before being declared ineligible to participate in a welfare program.

Unearned Income. Unearned income consists primarily of social security benefits, railroad retirement income, private pensions, interest, and dividends. In June 1976 about 70 percent of the aged SSI recipients received social security benefits averaging $138. Blind and disabled recipients were half as likely as the aged to receive social security but, when they did, their average monthly benefit was $139, approximately the same as the benefit for the aged. In addition, about 12 percent of the aged—as compared with 8 percent of the blind and 9 percent of the disabled—received types of unearned income other than social security.[16]

The first $20 of unearned income is disregarded in determining monthly SSI payments. This is about $12 more than the federal disregard under the old federal programs.[17] Unearned income not otherwise excluded is subtracted dollar for dollar from the SSI standard—that is, unearned income above $20 is taxed at an implicit rate of 100 percent. Thus, an SSI recipient with unearned income of $140 in July 1978 would have a total income of $209, as compared with a total of $189 for a counterpart with no other income.

Earned Income. The 1972 amendments permit SSI recipients to disregard the first $65 of monthly earnings ($85 for persons with no unearned income) plus half of any additional earnings in determining SSI payments.[18] This is substantially more than under previous federal

---

[15] The term "unearned" has pejorative connotations, and in common parlance is inappropriate when applied to certain types of nonwage income, such as interest and dividends.

[16] Unpublished data provided by the Social Security Administration.

[17] The income determination is made quarterly but is often expressed in monthly terms.

[18] SSI recipients may also disregard $10 a month of earned income and $20 a month of unearned income if received irregularly or infrequently.

programs and is more generous than the disregard for unearned income. To illustrate, in December 1978 a person with $145 in monthly wages and no other income could disregard $115—that is, $85 + 0.5 ($145 − $85)—as compared with $20 for an individual with $145 in social security income.

Break-Even Income. The break-even income is the level of income at which a person no longer qualifies for SSI payments.[19] Table 5 shows that the break-even level varies among SSI recipients depending upon the state in which they reside and the type of nonwelfare income they receive.[20] The first row in the table shows the amount paid to elderly persons with no other income. The second row shows the amount of social security income individuals must receive before they lose all SSI payments. The third row shows break-even income for persons with earned income only. The fourth and fifth rows show break-even levels for SSI recipients with both earned and unearned income: the greater the ratio of earnings to nonwelfare income, the greater the break-even level for SSI eligibility.

Even though SSI recipients can earn some income without losing SSI payments, Table 6 shows that in December 1975 fewer than 3 percent of the recipients had any earnings from employment. This rate is one and a half times as high as it was previously, with new recipients having an employment rate of 3.9 percent versus 1.8 percent for transferred recipients. Hence, it seems clear that the increase occurred not because formerly unemployed recipients found jobs to take advantage of the earnings disregard but because the rise in payment standards enabled working poor persons to qualify for assistance.

Aged recipients were less likely to work than the blind or disabled, partly because more than half of them were at least seventy-five years old. The aged who did work averaged less income than blind and disabled workers. Most worker-recipients appeared to benefit from the earnings disregard. Only 30 percent of them had more monthly income than allowed without penalty—in most cir-

---

[19] Break-even income (BI) for the ith recipient group in the jth state can be calculated by the following equation:

$$BI_{ij} = du + de + 2\ (SSI_{ij}),$$

where du is the unearned disregard, de equals the earnings disregard, and SSI_{ij} represents the combined federal-state payment standard for basic needs.

[20] More precisely, the break-even level of income within a state is the same for everyone with a specific type of income, but it can vary by income type between states.

TABLE 5

BREAK-EVEN LEVEL OF INCOME FOR THE BASIC NEEDS OF AGED INDIVIDUALS AND COUPLES, FEDERAL STANDARDS AND STANDARDS FOR SELECTED STATES, JULY 1, 1977

(dollars)

Type of Income	Federal Standard		California		New Jersey		Wisconsin	
	Individuals	Couples	Individuals	Couples	Individuals	Couples	Individuals	Couples
No other income[a]	178	267	296	557	200	277	254	386
Social security only	198	287	316	577	220	297	274	406
Earnings only	441	618	677	1,199	485	639	593	857
Social security and earnings[b]	301	398	537	979	345	419	453	637
Social security and earnings[c]	—[d]	—[d]	497	919	305	—[d]	413	577

NOTE: Income levels are rounded to the nearest dollar.

[a] For persons with no other income, the amounts shown represent actual SSI income rather than break-even income.

[b] Social security income of $160 for individuals and $240 for couples. Maximum earnings are: federal, $141 and $158; California, $377 and $739; New Jersey, $185 and $179; and Wisconsin, $293 and $397.

[c] Social security income of $200 for individuals and $300 for couples. Maximum earnings are: California, $297 and $619; New Jersey, $105; and Wisconsin, $213 and $277.

[d] Ineligible for SSI payments.

SOURCE: Author's calculations.

TABLE 6

NUMBER EMPLOYED AND EARNINGS OF SSI RECIPIENTS, DECEMBER 1975

Item	All Categories	Aged	Blind	Disabled
Number employed	114,483[a]	58,906	4,569	51,008
Percent of recipients	2.8	2.6	6.6	2.9
Average monthly earnings (dollars)	74.52	63.48	232.34	73.07

NOTE: Includes recipients with federally administered payments.

[a] Excludes 1,134 blind and disabled children who were employed.

SOURCE: Social Security Administration, "Employment and Earnings of SSI Beneficiaries, December 1975," *Research and Statistics Note*, note 4 (March 23, 1977), table 1.

cumstances it was less than $25. Overall, about 90 percent of all earned income was disregarded in calculating SSI payments.[21]

SSI income disregards are independent of household size. Thus, if an SSI couple receives social security benefits or other income, each spouse actually receives half the disregard they would have received if they were single. Moreover, the amount of income disregarded by the federal SSI program has not been adjusted for cost-of-living increases since the program began. This has resulted in a drop in the real income of many SSI recipients with social security and other types of income. For example, assume that the federal SSI standard of $178 and social security benefits are boosted by 10 percent. If a recipient with both SSI and social security income had initial social security benefits of $150 and the SSI increase is entirely passed along by the state, the recipient winds up with a gross income of $216, or only 9.1 percent more than his previous income of $198.[22]

In-Kind Income. In general, the aged, blind, and disabled receive reduced SSI payments if they receive in-kind support and maintenance

[21] Estimates based on Social Security Administration, "Employment and Earnings of SSI Beneficiaries, December 1975," *Research and Statistics Note*, note 4 (March 23, 1977), tables 1 and 4. Open-ended intervals closed by fitting a Pareto curve to the data. See U.S. Bureau of the Census, *Trends in the Income of Families and Persons in the United States, 1947–1964*, Technical Paper no. 17 (1967), pp. 32–36.

[22] The $198 is the sum of $150 social security and $48 SSI income. The $216 equals the sum of $165 (1.10 × $150) and $50.80 SSI income [(1.10 × $178) − ($165 − $20)].

17

from other persons. The reduction is no greater than one-third of the payment standard applicable to the individual. Hence, many SSI recipients are better off by accepting in-kind income from their children rather than money, since SSI payments are not reduced commensurately.

Limitations on Assets

Besides satisfying income criteria, persons eligible for SSI must meet resource requirements. These requirements prevent persons with large amounts of assets other than a home from receiving SSI payments. In general, federal law permits an individual to own no more than $1,500 ($2,250 for a couple) in assets other than a home and still receive SSI payments. This ceiling excludes personal possessions worth up to $1,500, an automobile with a market value under $1,200, and a life insurance policy with a face value less than $1,500.[23] In addition, certain property indispensable for self-support (tools or business assets) and resources that the handicapped need for self-support are excluded. To receive an optional supplementary payment, an individual must comply with any additional state requirements. In January 1977 several states had resource exclusions that differed from the federal exclusions.[24]

Persons eligible for SSI can own a home and still receive cash assistance. Since October 1976 there has been no limit on the value of a home an individual can own and still qualify for welfare payments. Before 1976 the SSI limit was $25,000 ($35,000 in Alaska and Hawaii). Under previous welfare programs, the limit tended to be lower, and many states required a lien against real property as a condition of eligibility. This probably discouraged many needy people from applying for financial assistance. SSI abolished lien requirements for federal payments but permits state-administered programs to impose them for entitlement to state supplements.

A home is the asset most frequently reported by persons who became eligible for welfare after the advent of SSI. In June 1976 almost 25 percent of all SSI households owned homes. The homeownership rate among aged individuals was 29 percent, as compared

---

[23] Many persons are denied eligibility because instead of life insurance they have excessive savings that are earmarked for funeral expenses. It has been recommended that consideration be given to "making the $1,500 insurance policy exclusion alternatively available with respect to amounts in a burial fund." See Senate, Committee on Finance, *The Supplemental Security Income Program*, p. 82.
[24] Social Security Administration, "State Supplementary Payment Provisions under SSI," pp. 6–8.

with about 15 percent among the blind and disabled. In several states more than 30 percent of the aged and disabled households owned a home—42 percent in New Mexico and 38 percent in Arkansas and Mississippi.[25] Because the implicit income from home ownership is not included in countable income in determining SSI payments, homeowners may receive much larger incomes than nonhomeowners but still receive identical SSI payments.

Differences in resource limitations are likely to affect personal preferences for assets. SSI resource exclusions favor home ownership and discourage holding wealth in cash or other financial assets. Thus, some households have an incentive to become eligible for SSI payments by transferring excess assets to friends or relatives, purchasing a house, or modernizing their present residence. There is an additional incentive to purchase or modernize a home if a state makes optional supplementary payments for special housing needs and permits the individual to will the house to heirs without reimbursing the state for the supplementary payments.

Eligibility for Food Stamps

Under 1973 welfare programs, aged, blind, and disabled persons were eligible for food stamps and surplus commodities.[26] Although participation in the food stamp program was generally low, welfare recipients were permitted to purchase stamps at prices that varied with income: the poorer the recipient, the larger the bonus value of the stamps—that is, the difference between their face value and their purchase price.

The 1972 amendments stipulated that SSI recipients would not be eligible for food stamps and surplus commodities. Grandfathered recipients were not expected to be affected adversely by this change since the increase in the payment received because of SSI was larger than the food stamp bonus. In some states, the federal SSI standard was significantly higher than the former standard. Where it was not, the states were expected to offset the difference by supplementary payments. This expectation was legally mandated in August 1973 in response to congressional concern over the possibility of inadequate supplementation. This mandate requires "a retroactive, retrospective

---

[25] Social Security Administration, "Financial Assets of New SSI Beneficiaries," *Research and Statistics Note,* note 17 (October 3, 1977), tables 1 and 2.

[26] For a discussion of the food stamp program, see Congressional Budget Office, *The Food Stamp Program: Income or Food Supplementation?* (January 1977).

look at what would have happened had SSI never been enacted."[27] In other words, a recipient would be eligible for food stamps if the SSI payment was less than the bonus value of the food stamps plus the payment the individual could have received in December 1973.

The day before SSI was inaugurated, the loss of food stamp eligibility was deferred for six months because of the extreme administrative difficulties surrounding the legislation of August 1973. This deferral did not affect the five states (California, Massachusetts, Nevada, New York, and Wisconsin) that had increased their supplementary standards by adding $10 per recipient to replace the bonus value of food stamps. In the other states and the District of Columbia, SSI recipients remained eligible for food stamps until July 1, 1974.[28] This suspension has been extended several times with each postponement usually being for one year. Nevada and New York reestablished food stamps for SSI recipients in 1976. In late 1978, over 1.2 million SSI recipients received food stamps.

Administration

The Social Security Administration has administrative responsibility for federal SSI payments. It makes eligibility determinations and redeterminations, issues monthly checks, maintains the records of recipients, and pays for administrative costs. Formerly, the states administered the programs, established payment levels, and made eligibility determinations.

Mandatory and optional state supplementary payments may be administered by either the federal government or the state.[29] The 1972 amendments permit each state to elect federal administration of the supplements and gives the states financial incentives to do so, including federal assumption of administrative costs.[30] Any state electing federal administration of its optional supplements must automatically elect

---

[27] U.S. Congress, House of Representatives, Subcommittee on Public Assistance of the Committee on Ways and Means, *Extension of Interim Assistance and Food Stamps for SSI Beneficiaries and Continuation of Federal-State Matching Funds for Non-Welfare Recipient Children,* 94th Congress, 2nd session, June 10, 1976, p. 3.

[28] Social Security Administration, "Food Stamp Eligibility for Supplemental Security Income Recipients," *Research and Statistics Note,* note 28 (September 30, 1974), p. 2.

[29] Social Security Administration, *The Supplemental Security Income Program for the Aged, Blind, and Disabled* (July 1978), pp. x–xii.

[30] The Social Security Administration is prohibited from administering optional supplementary payments for special needs. This is a responsibility of state and local governments.

federal administration of its mandatory payments, unless the state can justify doing otherwise. Once a state elects federal administration of the optional supplement, it must abide by federal rules and regulations.

Table A-1 in the Appendix shows that on July 1, 1978, twenty-six states and the District of Columbia had federal administration of the mandatory supplementary payments. The remaining states administered these payments themselves, except for Texas and West Virginia, where mandatory supplements were not paid. Sixteen of the twenty-six states with federally administered mandatory supplements also had federal administration of the optional payments. Southern and midwestern states, in general, were more likely than northeastern states to elect state administration or not to make supplementary payments. For example, half of the eight states that make up Region IV of the United States elected federally administered mandatory supplements, whereas none chose federal administration of the optional payments. Four of the six Region I states, however, had federal administration of both supplements.[31]

---

[31] The secretary of health, education, and welfare could refuse to administer state supplementary standards that are inconsistent with the goals of nationwide uniformity and program simplicity. The secretary has reportedly issued regulations permitting the Social Security Administration to administer many different payment levels. Staff of the Senate Committee on Finance believe that these regulations and related policies "have unduly complicated the administration of the program, and been responsible in large part for the inability to complete work on acceptably functioning systems." See U.S. Congress, House of Representatives, Committee on Ways and Means, *Social Security Amendments of 1971*, 92nd Congress, 1st session, May 26, 1971, p. 200; and Senate, Committee on Finance, *The Supplemental Security Income Program*, p. 71.

2

The Effects of SSI on Recipients

The impact of SSI on the incomes of the aged, blind, and disabled can be measured by the number of recipients, the recipient rate, total payments, the average monthly payment per recipient, and annual per capita expenditures. Each measure reflects a certain aspect of the extent to which financial assistance reaches target populations. Together, they portray a relatively complete picture of the impact of SSI on the individuals the program is designed to help.

Historical experience suggests that a portion of the changes in each measure following the introduction of SSI would have occurred if SSI had not been enacted.[1] Consequently, raw or unadjusted comparisons of data before and after SSI may misrepresent the true impact of SSI. Comparisons of dollar amounts might, for example, overstate SSI's effect on welfare income because the states might have increased welfare payments at a faster rate than in the past in light of the abnormally high rate of inflation of the mid-1970s. On the other hand, during this period the states might have curtailed increases in welfare payments because of the need to finance alternative social programs, the 1974–1975 recession, the increase in social security benefits, or more liberal eligibility requirements for Medicaid and food stamps.

---

[1] Munnell and Connolly estimate that about half the increase in aggregate payments is directly attributable to SSI. See Alicia H. Munnell and Ann M. Connolly, "Federalizing Welfare: The Fiscal Impact of the SSI Program," *New England Economic Review* (September-October 1977), p. 13. For estimates of the caseload increase without SSI, see Sylvester J. Schieber, "The Dynamics of the Adult Assistance Caseload and the Impact of the Supplemental Security Income Program" (paper presented at the meetings of the Eastern Economic Association, April 27–29, 1978).

TABLE 7

Number of Public Assistance and SSI Recipients and Total Amount of Public Assistance and SSI Payments, by Recipient Group, Selected Years

Item[a]	Public Assistance				SSI		
	1965	1971	1973	1974	1975	1976	1977
Number of recipients (thousands)[a, b]							
Aged	2,099	2,035	1,801	2,314	2,334	2,176	2,078
Disabled	555	978	1,258	1,650	1,951	2,034	2,132
Blind	93	80	77	76	75	77	78
Total	2,747	3,093	3,136	4,040[c]	4,360[c]	4,287[c]	4,288[c]
Total payments (millions of dollars)							
Aged	1,591	1,883	1,739	2,504	2,605	2,505	2,448
Disabled	415	1,186	1,607	2,612	3,142	3,425	3,710
Blind	77	101	104	130	131	138	146
Total	2,083	3,170	3,450	5,246[d]	5,878[d]	6,068[d]	6,304[d]

Note: Excludes Guam, Puerto Rico, and the U.S. Virgin Islands.

[a] December of each year.

[b] About 10 percent of the SSI blind and disabled recipients were aged sixty-five and over. Percentage differed under pre-SSI programs.

[c] Partly estimated. Includes persons with federal SSI payments, federally administered state supplements, or state-administered state supplements.

[d] Partly estimated.

Sources: *Social Security Bulletin* and *Supplemental Security Income for the Aged, Blind, and Disabled*, Monthly Statistics, various issues; and unpublished data provided by the Social Security Administration.

Number of Recipients

As Table 7 shows, between 1973 and 1974 the number of aged, blind, and disabled recipients rose to 4 million, a gain of 29 percent compared with almost no change during the previous two years. The number of recipients grew by an additional 320,000 (7.9 percent) in 1975; in 1976 and 1977 the number dipped by 72,000 to 4.29 million recipients. This decline was partly the result of increases in social security benefits raising the income of many people above the eligibility levels for SSI payments.

In December 1978 about 60 percent of SSI recipients received a federal SSI payment only, while 28 percent received both a federal and a state supplementary SSI payment.[2] Twelve percent of the recipients had too much countable income to receive federal SSI payments, but they did receive a state supplement. Blind and disabled recipients were more likely than the aged to receive both a federal and a state payment and less likely to have a state supplementary payment only. This is not surprising since aged recipients generally averaged more nonwelfare income than blind and disabled recipients.

As shown in Table 8, the change in the number of recipients varied substantially across states. For example, between December 1973 and December 1977 the number of aged recipients in Louisiana fell by 22 percent, as compared with an increase of 143 percent in Wisconsin. Similarly, the change in the number of disabled recipients ranged from 11 percent in Illinois to 223 percent in Texas.

Projections in Recipient Growth. The increase in the total number of recipients is considerably below the projection of the Social Security Administration, which expected that the number of aged, blind, and disabled recipients would nearly double to 6.1 million with the inception of the SSI program.[3] In January 1974, the first month of the program, only 3.2 million persons received federally administered payments—an increase of only 200,000 persons above the number receiving cash assistance in December 1973.[4] The number of aged

---

[2] Estimated from Social Security Administration, *Supplemental Security Income for the Aged, Blind, and Disabled*, Quarterly Statistics (December 1978), table 1, and Monthly Statistics (February 1979), table 12.

[3] Social Security Administration, "Supplemental Security Income: A Preliminary Look at the Aged Eligible," *Research and Statistics Note*, note 10 (May 22, 1973). The Social Security Administration assumed that 10 percent of the eligible population would not participate in the new program.

[4] James C. Callison, "Early Experience under the Supplemental Security Income Program," *Social Security Bulletin*, vol. 37 (June 1974), pp. 3–12.

TABLE 8

NUMBER OF AGED, BLIND, AND DISABLED RECIPIENTS, SELECTED STATES AND YEARS

(thousands of persons)

State	Aged Recipients				Disabled Recipients				Total Recipients			
	1973	1975	1977	Percent change 1973–1977	1973	1975	1977	Percent change 1973–1977	1973	1975	1977	Percent change 1973–1977
United States	1,801	2,334	2,078	15.4	1,258	1,951	2,132	69.5	3,136	4,360	4,288	36.7
Alabama[a]	106	104	93	−12.3	21	45	51	142.9	129	152	146	13.2
California	286	334	326	14.0	219	318	350	59.8	519	666	693	33.5
Georgia	82	94	82	0.0	40	69	75	87.5	125	165	161	28.8
Illinois[a]	31	50	43	38.7	84	96	93	10.7	116	148	138	19.0
Louisiana	102	94	80	−21.6	25	56	66	164.0	129	152	148	14.7
Massachusetts	57	81	74	29.8	30	48	51	70.0	90	132	130	44.4
New York	106	179	154	45.3	175	220	225	28.6	285	403	384	34.7
Ohio	43	54	44	2.3	51	75	79	54.9	96	132	126	31.3
Texas	170	191	169	−0.6	31	85	100	222.6	205	280	273	33.2
Wisconsin	14	37	34	142.9	10	28	32	220.0	24	66	67	179.2

NOTE: Number of recipients is for December of each year and includes persons with a federal SSI payment, a federally administered state supplement, or a state-administered supplement.

[a] Partly estimated.

SOURCES: Social Security Administration, *Supplemental Security Income for the Aged, Blind, and Disabled, Monthly Statistics* (February 1976), table 10, and *Program and Demographic Characteristics of Supplemental Security Beneficiaries* (December 1975), table 2; and Appendix, table A-2, in this volume.

recipients in January 1974 (1.9 million) was approximately half the official projection. Moreover, as of December 1978, the total recipient population had never exceeded 4.4 million nor had the number of aged recipients been greater than 2.4 million.

The increase in the number of blind and disabled recipients has been much larger than forecasted. The Social Security Administration estimated that the number of these recipients would rise from 1.2 million in December 1972 to 1.8 million in January 1974. Aged SSI recipients were expected to outnumber the disabled and blind by two to one. In December 1978, 2.3 million disabled and blind persons received assistance, as compared with 2.0 million aged people.

Despite the rapid growth in the number of disabled SSI recipients, it is sometimes claimed that the disability criteria are too severe and inappropriate for the people SSI is designed to help.[5] For example, the work-related criteria, particularly the twelve-month standard, is said to prevent many alcoholics and drug addicts from receiving assistance because their condition does not keep them from gainful employment.[6]

Several reasons have been advanced to explain the inaccurate forecasts of the number of SSI recipients. The census data used to make the projections may have been inadequate. Also, eligible people may still be unaware of the SSI program, while some may have had their applications for SSI incorrectly disapproved.

A telephone survey of Social Security Administration district offices cast doubt upon the view that a large number of eligible people are unaware of the SSI program.[7] Further, a mail survey of the states found that more than half the respondents believed that potentially eligible aged persons knew about the program; fewer than half felt a large proportion of eligible persons was uninformed. The respond-

---

[5] To qualify for SSI disability assistance, a person must satisfy similar medical and work-related requirements as a person qualifying for disability benefits under social security. An individual must be unable to engage in any substantial gainful activity because of a medically determined physical or mental condition that is expected to last at least twelve consecutive months or result in death. Under prior disability welfare programs, the medical eligibility criteria varied by state and sometimes were less restrictive than the SSI definition.

[6] About 2,600 alcoholics and 7,500 drug addicts received disability SSI payments in February 1976, up from 9,800 in December 1973. See Social Security Administration, "SSI Beneficiaries Medically Determined to Be Alcoholics or Drug Addicts," *Research and Statistics Note*, note 8 (June 7, 1977), table 3. In addition to meeting work criteria, alcoholics or drug addicts must undergo and adhere to rehabilitative treatment in an approved facility in order to be eligible for SSI payments. All SSI payments for alcoholics and drug addicts are made to representative payees.

[7] U.S. Congress, Senate, Committee on Finance, *The Supplemental Security Income Program*, 95th Congress, 1st session, April 1977, pp. 104–6.

ents, however, thought that a large number of disabled children were unaware of their SSI eligibility.

Concerning the possibility that applications may have been incorrectly turned down, a 1974 Social Security Administration study concluded that this "does not appear to be any major area of deficiency."[8] A study by the Department of Health, Education, and Welfare of 2,000 cases in which the Social Security Administration claims representatives were asked to explain the basis for their rejections concluded that only 3.8 percent of the disallowances were unwarranted. If this percentage is projected over all disallowances, an estimated 30,000 persons a year may have been denied assistance they were entitled to receive.[9]

The unexpectedly low number of SSI recipients has resulted in substantial criticism of the Social Security Administration's efforts to inform the public about the program. Nevertheless, the amount spent to publicize the program has actually been very large—$8 million by the Administration on Aging between 1973 and 1974, and $16.7 million by the Social Security Administration for fiscal years 1974 through 1976.[10] Besides mass media campaigns, these outlays financed the SSI Alert between November 1973 and June 1974, in which 50,000 community and neighborhood volunteers were recruited to canvass isolated individuals and minorities who might be eligible for assistance. In addition, between 1974 and 1975 the Social Security Administration screened and contacted everyone on the social security files who might have been eligible for SSI.[11]

Recipient Characteristics. As Table 9 shows, in 1977 more than half the aged recipients were over seventy-four years of age. Also, a large

---

[8] Ibid.

[9] Between January 1974 and June 1975, the Social Security Administration made eligibility determinations for 3 million new applications. Slightly more than 2 million were approved for a federally administered SSI payment, inclusive of applicants initially declared ineligible but subsequently approved following appeals to reconsider their claims. Aged applicants were more likely than allegedly blind and disabled persons to receive approval—85 percent versus 55 percent. Aged persons were more likely to be disapproved because of excess income or resources. Allegedly blind and disabled applicants ordinarily were rejected because their impairment was medically determined to lack severity for disability assistance or because they were judged able to engage in substantial gainful activity. See Social Security Administration, "Denials under the Supplemental Security Income Program, January 1974–July 1975," *Research and Statistics Note*, note 26 (December 16, 1976), table 1.

[10] U.S. Congress, House of Representatives, Subcommittee on Oversight of the Committee on Ways and Means, *Oversight of the Supplemental Security Income Program*, 94th Congress, 2nd session, April 8 and May 6, 1976, pp. 144–45.

[11] Ibid., p. 145.

TABLE 9

PERCENTAGE DISTRIBUTION OF AGED, BLIND, AND DISABLED RECIPIENTS
WITH PUBLIC ASSISTANCE OR SSI PAYMENTS, SELECTED
CHARACTERISTICS, 1973 AND 1977

Characteristic	Aged 1973	Aged 1977[a]	Blind 1973	Blind 1977[a]	Disabled 1973	Disabled 1977[a]
Age (years)						
18–29	0.0	0.0	9.3	16.6	11.5	15.9
30–49	0.0	0.0	19.6	19.9	26.2	24.8
50–64	0.0	0.0	34.3	28.6	58.8	45.0
65–74	48.1	44.9	17.1	17.8	3.2	14.0
75 and over	51.9	55.1	19.6	17.1	0.2	0.3
All ages[b]	100.0[c]	100.0	100.0[c]	100.0	100.0[c]	100.0
Sex						
Male	30.3	28.5	49.6	44.0	44.3	40.6
Female	69.7	71.4	50.4	56.0	55.7	59.4
Both sexes	100.0	100.0	100.0	100.0	100.0	100.0
Race						
White	63.3	65.4	60.0	63.6	60.6	64.8
Black	26.1	24.6	30.8	28.8	30.5	29.8
Other	2.5	3.2	2.5	3.1	2.7	2.8
Not reported	8.1	6.8	6.6	4.5	6.2	2.6
All races	100.0[d]	100.0	100.0[d]	100.0	100.0[d]	100.0
Residence						
Metropolitan area	57.3	56.7	64.9	65.3	71.7	69.2
Nonmetropolitan area	42.7	43.3	35.1	34.7	28.3	30.8
Both areas	100.0[d]	100.0[e]	100.0[d]	100.0[e]	100.0[d]	100.0[e]
Living arrangement						
Own household	89.1	87.9	88.9	86.5	85.1	82.6
Another's household	6.9	7.6	7.8	9.5	9.6	11.7
Medicaid institution	4.0	4.5	3.3	4.0	5.3	5.8
All arrangements	100.0[f]	100.0	100.0[f]	100.0	100.0[f]	100.0

NOTE: Detail may not add to total because of rounding.

[a] Recipients with a federally administered payment.

[b] Excludes blind and disabled recipients under eighteen years of age.

[c] Data for January 1970.

[d] Transferred recipients.

[e] Data for December 1974.

[f] Data for May 1974.

SOURCES: Lenna D. Kennedy and others, "Conversions to Supplemental Security Income from State Assistance: A Program Records Study," *Social Security Bul-*

proportion of the blind and disabled recipients were relatively old: about 60 percent of them were over forty-nine years of age and more than 14 percent were at least sixty-five years of age.

Aged recipients were more likely to be female than were the blind or the disabled. Whites constituted more than 63 percent of each recipient group in 1977, about three percentage points higher than in 1973. A larger proportion of the newly awarded recipients were white rather than nonwhite. For example, in June 1975, 68.4 percent of the newly awarded aged recipients were white, as compared with 63.3 percent of the transferred recipients. That this occurred is not surprising. Since whites generally have larger incomes than nonwhites, an increase in payment levels can be expected to add relatively more whites to the welfare rolls than nonwhites.

The proportion of recipients living in metropolitan areas declined between 1973 and 1975 because a higher proportion of newly awarded recipients lived outside metropolitan areas. In the case of the disabled, 38 percent of the new awardees resided in a nonmetropolitan area, as compared with 28 percent of the transferred recipients. This residential shift may be attributable to the outreach efforts of the Social Security Administration to enroll eligible rural persons in the SSI program.

Almost 88 percent of the aged recipients lived in their own homes in 1977; that is, they were sole or joint household heads or they resided in a domiciliary care facility. In general, blind and disabled recipients were more likely than the aged to reside in another's home or in a Medicaid institution because of their greater difficulty living independently.

Recipient Rates

Tables 10 and 11 show recipient rates for the aged and disabled. A recipient rate indicates a target group's participation in a program,

letin, vol. 38 (June 1975), table 10; Social Security Administration, "Distribution of Beneficiaries under the SSI Program, by Race, June 1975," Research and Statistics Note, note 25 (December 15, 1976), table E; U.S. Department of Health, Education, and Welfare, Findings of the 1970 AB Study, pt. 1 (September 1972), table 1; Findings of the 1970 APTD Study, pt. 1 (September 1972), table 1; Findings of the 1970 OAA Study, pt. 1 (September 1972), table 1; Social Security Administration, "Payments, Social Security Benefits, and Living Arrangements under the Supplemental Security Income Program," Research and Statistics Note, note 36 (December 20, 1974), table 5; Social Security Administration, Program and Demographic Characteristics of Supplemental Security Beneficiaries, December 1975 (1978), various tables; and Social Security Administration, "SSI Beneficiaries Residing in Urban Areas," Research and Statistics Note, note 8 (April 27, 1976), table 1.

TABLE 10

PUBLIC ASSISTANCE AND SSI RECIPIENT RATES, AVERAGE MONTHLY PAYMENT PER RECIPIENT, AND ANNUAL PER CAPITA EXPENDITURE, BY RECIPIENT GROUP, SELECTED YEARS

Year	Recipient Rate		Average Monthly Payment per Recipient (dollars)			Annual per Capita Expenditure (dollars)	
	Aged[a]	Disabled[b]	Aged	Blind	Disabled	Aged	Disabled
1965	115	5.0	62.70	68.41	64.21	86.20	3.89
1971	98	8.5	77.50	105.74	99.82	91.55	10.21
1973	85	10.0	79.67	111.97	111.66	81.53	13.36
1974[c]	98	12.1	97.36	144.44	147.58	114.78	21.36
1975[c]	104	14.8	92.78	145.74	142.66	116.27	25.26
1976[c]	98	16.0	93.13	148.01	140.91	109.23	27.07
1977[c]	90	16.3	96.62	156.79	147.76	104.20	28.85

NOTE: Recipients and population data for July of each year.

[a] Number of recipients per 1,000 persons aged sixty-five and over.

[b] Number of recipients per 1,000 persons aged eighteen to sixty-four.

[c] Partly estimated.

SOURCES: Author's calculations. Recipient and payment information from various issues of the *Social Security Bulletin* and *Social Security Administration, Supplemental Security Income for the Aged, Blind, and Disabled*, Monthly Statistics. Population figures from U.S. Bureau of the Census, *Current Population Reports*, Series P-25.

TABLE 11

RECIPIENT RATES FOR AGED AND DISABLED PERSONS, SELECTED STATES, 1973 AND 1977

State	Aged Rate[a]		Disabled Rate[b]	
	1973	1977	1973	1977
United States	85	90	10.0	16.3
Alabama	303	237	10.0	23.4
California	149	149	16.9	25.8
Connecticut	23	30	5.7	9.3
Iowa	31	37	2.0	7.5
Mississippi	336	275	22.5	34.1
New Hampshire	32	28	3.1	5.2
New Jersey	26	43	4.8	10.0
New York	55	74	15.3	20.5
Texas	158	140	4.2	12.8
Wyoming	36	31	4.3	4.5

NOTE: Recipients and population data for July of each year.
[a] Number of recipients per 1,000 persons aged sixty-five and over.
[b] Number of recipients per 1,000 persons aged eighteen to sixty-four.
SOURCES: Appendix, Tables A-3 and A-4.

with participation determined by receipt of a cash payment, irrespective of its amount. The aged recipient rate represents the number of recipients sixty-five years and older per 1,000 persons of that age. The disabled recipient rate shows the number of disabled recipients per 1,000 persons aged eighteen to sixty-four years.[12] A separate rate is not shown for the blind because of the comparatively small number of such recipients.

As shown in Table 10, recipient rates increased considerably after the advent of SSI. For the aged, SSI halted a decline that had occurred between 1965 and 1973. In 1975, 10.4 percent of persons aged sixty-five and over received assistance payments, as compared with 8.5 percent in 1973. In 1976 the rate dipped to its 1974 level;

---

[12] This base was used because of the unavailability of data showing the number of potentially eligible disabled recipients. The same base was used in Lora S. Collins, "Public Assistance Expenditures in the United States," in Otto Eckstein, ed., *Studies in the Economics of Income Maintenance* (Washington, D.C.: Brookings Institution, 1967), pp. 97–173. The Department of Health, Education, and Welfare has used the entire population for the disability base. This was not done here because of the comparatively small number of disabled recipients who are sixty-five and over, or under eighteen.

it fell below that level in 1977. One reason for the decline is that many aged persons who had been marginally eligible for SSI in 1975 subsequently lost their eligibility as their social security income increased at a faster rate than SSI standards.[13]

The disabled recipient rate doubled between 1965 and 1973 because of the expansion of the welfare program for permanently and totally disabled persons. SSI accelerated the growth in the disabled recipient rate from 9 percent a year between 1965 and 1973 to 13 percent a year during the next four years.

Increased recipient rates were accompanied by a rise in the number of dual recipients—persons concurrently receiving welfare payments and social security benefits. From 1973 to 1977 the number of aged SSI recipients who were dual recipients rose from 67 percent to 70 percent. The proportion of dual disabled recipients rose much more—from 24 percent to 35 percent. Although dual recipiency provides additional income for needy persons, it may have adverse effects on the payoff for social security taxes (see Chapter 6).

Recipient rates vary considerably among states, but the ranges narrowed after SSI was implemented. As shown in Table 11, in 1977 the aged recipient rate varied from 28 per 1,000 persons in New Hampshire to 275 per 1,000 persons in Mississippi; the disability recipient rate, from 4.5 per 1,000 persons in Wyoming to approximately 34 per 1,000 persons in Mississippi. These interstate differences may be the result of differences in the number of needy aged and disabled people, payment standards, and the willingness to apply for and accept welfare payments.

Total Payments

Table 7 reports that aggregate welfare payments for the aged, blind, and disabled increased by 52 percent between 1973 and 1974, as compared with average annual increases of 6.5 percent between 1965 and 1973. After 1974, the annual rate of increase in SSI payments declined to 12 percent in 1974–1975, 3 percent in 1975–1976, and 4 percent in 1976–1977. SSI payments for the aged decreased after the second year of the program, but they increased for the disabled. The trend of payments in a selected group of states is shown for 1973 to 1977 in Table 12. There are wide differences among the states. The payments

[13] Social Security Administration figures show that in July 1975 about 66,200 persons became ineligible for SSI because of increases in social security benefits. See House of Representatives, Subcommittee on Oversight of the Committee on Ways and Means, *Oversight of the Supplemental Security Income Program*, p. 140.

to disabled persons, for example, increased fourfold in Texas, as compared with a 38 percent increase in Illinois.

Average Monthly Payment per Recipient

The monthly SSI payment is the amount paid after countable wages, social security benefits, and other income are deducted from the payment standard. Since some income is usually deducted in calculating payments, the trend in payments may differ from the trend in total income. As a result, changes in this measure may not adequately reflect the impact of SSI on the economic well-being of the aged, blind, and disabled.

As Table 10 shows, the monthly payment for a typical person in each recipient group increased between 1965 and 1973. Blind and disabled recipients almost always averaged higher monthly payments than the aged, and their monthly payment increased at a faster rate during those years. Monthly payments increased sharply during the first year of the SSI program but declined for the aged and disabled in 1975. Overall, between 1973 and 1977 the average monthly payment for aged recipients increased by 21 percent, as compared with an increase of 40 percent for the blind and 32 percent for the disabled.

Both the level of, and the change in, the monthly payments for aged recipients were less than amounts for blind and disabled recipients. The primary explanation is that aged recipients averaged more non-SSI income, particularly social security benefits, than other recipients. For example, 71 percent of the rise in the typical aged recipient's estimated gross income from $126 in January 1970 to $188 in December 1975 was attributable to increases in social security benefits. The comparable figure for the disabled was 32 percent of the rise from $119 to $194.[14]

In Table 13, the average monthly payment per aged recipient in 1973 in the continental U.S. ranges from $55 in Mississippi to $113 in Wisconsin. Four years later the range is somewhat wider but at a higher level—from $60 in Maine to $138 in California. In the case of disabled recipients, the relative difference is considerably narrower, although the absolute difference increases slightly. In 1977, the payment for the disabled ranged from $103 in Kansas to $204 in California.

[14] U.S. Department of Health, Education, and Welfare, *Findings of the 1970 OAA Study* and *Findings of the APTD Study*, pt. 2 (December 1972), computed from various tables; Social Security Administration, *Program and Demographic Characteristics*, various tables.

TABLE 12

Total Expenditures for Public Assistance and SSI Payments for the Aged, Blind, and Disabled, Selected States and Years

(millions of dollars)

State	Aged				Disabled				Total Payments			
	1973	1975	1977	Percent change 1973–1977	1973	1975	1977	Percent change 1973–1977	1973	1975	1977	Percent change 1973–1977
United States	1,738.6	2,604.8	2,448.3	42.3	1,606.5	3,142.3	3,709.5	130.9	3,449.6	5,878.2	6,304.3	83.8
Alabama[a]	95.4	105.2	97.6	2.3	19.3	57.1	72.2	274.1	117.2	163.0	172.9	47.5
California	386.9	518.8	538.0	39.1	379.0	705.3	850.7	124.5	793.7	1,256.3	1,432.1	80.4
Georgia	58.3	90.6	82.8	42.0	33.4	82.7	103.1	208.7	94.5	177.6	190.3	101.4
Illinois[a]	26.7	47.8	44.6	67.0	112.9	149.2	156.0	38.2	141.8	200.1	203.4	43.4
Massachusetts	74.3	124.9	101.5	36.6	50.8	102.1	104.7	106.1	130.4	234.8	217.1	66.5
Mississippi	53.4	79.2	73.5	37.6	21.9	55.3	66.8	205.0	77.0	137.4	143.2	86.0
New York	131.6	229.9	205.3	56.0	289.0	449.1	459.3	58.9	427.1	687.7	672.4	57.4
Ohio	33.2	48.0	41.9	26.2	50.9	104.5	119.1	134.0	86.6	156.0	164.5	90.0
Texas	114.1	172.7	160.3	40.5	26.4	96.2	130.3	393.6	144.2	274.5	296.5	105.6
Wisconsin	26.1	44.2	38.3	46.7	13.9	43.3	55.3	297.8	40.9	89.1	95.3	133.0

[a] Partly estimated.

SOURCE: Social Security Administration, *Supplemental Security Income for the Aged, Blind, and Disabled,* Monthly Statistics (February 1976), table 10, and *Program and Demographic Characteristics of Supplemental Security Beneficiaries* (December 1975), table 2; and Appendix Table A-5 in this volume.

TABLE 13

AVERAGE MONTHLY PUBLIC ASSISTANCE PAYMENT IN 1973 AND AVERAGE SSI PAYMENT IN 1977 PER AGED AND DISABLED RECIPIENT, SELECTED STATES
(dollars)

State	Aged		Disabled	
	1973	1977	1973	1977
United States	80	96	112	148
California	112	138	149	204
Georgia	59	82	69	117
Indiana	58	68	59	111
Kansas	63	71	81	103
Maine	75	60	108	113
Massachusetts	109	115	152	177
Michigan	72	102	116	154
Mississippi	55	84	65	125
New York	101	110	147	173
Wisconsin	113	94	117	146

SOURCES: Appendix, Tables A-3 and A-4.

Annual per Capita Expenditure

The recipient rate measures the breadth of coverage, whereas the monthly payment indicates the depth of coverage. Annual per capita expenditures capture both breadth and depth because they depend upon the number of persons receiving assistance as well as the amount received. Annual per capita expenditures would be unaffected if opposite changes in the two components are counterbalancing.

As Table 10 shows, annual per capita expenditures for aged persons were lower in 1973 than in 1965 (the decrease in the aged recipient rate outweighed the increase in the monthly payment per aged recipient) but rose 28 percent between 1973 and 1977. For the blind and disabled, the combined increase in the recipient rate and monthly payment per recipient more than doubled annual per capita expenditures—from $13.36 in 1973 to $28.85 in 1977.

Table 14 shows a narrowing of the interstate differences in annual per capita expenditures for the aged and disabled. The preponderance of states with comparatively low payment standards among the states with high per capita expenditures is largely attributable to above-

35

TABLE 14

ANNUAL PER CAPITA EXPENDITURES FOR PUBLIC ASSISTANCE IN 1973 AND
SSI IN 1977, AGED AND DISABLED PERSONS, SELECTED STATES
(dollars)

State	Aged Persons		Disabled Persons	
	1973	1977	1973	1977
United States	82	104	13	29
Alabama	269	245	10	34
California	200	246	30	63
Indiana	19	27	3	9
Iowa	27	29	2	9
Louisiana	280	240	8	42
Massachusetts	114	148	15	30
Michigan	42	65	14	24
Mississippi	222	276	18	51
New York	66	99	27	43
Wyoming	29	27	4	6

SOURCES: Appendix, Tables A-3 and A-4.

average recipient rates in these states. For example, whereas southern
states generally had low payment standards in 1973 and provided
minimal state supplements in 1977, their recipient rates tended to be
markedly higher than those in other states.

Horizontal and Vertical Inequity

Under the old programs, each state established its own payment levels
and eligibility criteria. Since the states differed widely in their ability
and desire to finance welfare programs, there would be horizontal
inequities if persons with the same income were not treated equally
and if payment differences were not attributable to differences in the
cost of living. Although uniform federal SSI payment standards were
expected to alleviate such inequities, state supplementary programs
could have canceled their intended effects.[15]

---

[15] In 1972 the maximum monthly payment to a nonmarried elderly person who
had no countable income and lived independently varied from $75 in two counties
in Mississippi to $239 in Nassau County, New York. Similarly, the payment to an
aged couple ranged from $80 in Beaufort, South Carolina, to $414 in Contra Costa
County, California. See U.S. Congress, Subcommittee on Fiscal Policy of the

According to data presented in tables in this chapter, in both 1973 and 1977 the states varied considerably in recipient rates, payment standards, payments per recipient, and annual per capita expenditures. Nevertheless, as is indicated in Tables 11–14, there has been a narrowing in these differences. Table 15 shows that the coefficients of variation for the recipient rate, payment standards, average monthly payment per recipient, and annual per capita expenditures are lower in 1976 than 1973.[16] The standard deviations of logarithms and Gini coefficients are also lower in 1976 than 1973. Especially noticeable is the large drop in the standard deviations of logarithms for the payment standards. On the other hand, the constancy in the standard deviations of the monthly payments per recipient shown in Table 15 suggests no reduction in inequity, while the sharp rise in the deviations for annual per capita expenditures suggests greater inequity. The large decline in the standard deviations for payment standards, however, indicates less inequity for individuals with no other income.

Horizontal inequities could possibly be reduced by raising federal SSI standards so that no state would find it necessary to make supplementary payments. This would not necessarily eliminate inequities, however, unless allowances were made for interstate differences in living costs. Moreover, the cost of raising federal standards would be high. If, for instance, federal standards had been raised in 1977 to California's levels, SSI would have cost an additional $2.5 billion for current recipients, plus the amount that would have been spent for persons newly eligible for assistance because of the increase in payment levels.

Regardless of the federal standards, many states would probably provide supplementary payments because of cost-of-living differences

---

Joint Economic Committee, *The New Supplemental Security Income Program: Impact on Current Benefits and Unresolved Issues*, 93rd Congress, 1st session, paper no. 10, October 9, 1973, p. 11.

[16] Four statistics were calculated to determine whether horizontal inequities decreased between 1973 and 1976: the standard deviation, the coefficient of variation, the standard deviation of logarithms, and the Gini coefficient. Each statistic embodies a different notion of social welfare and makes an implicit assumption about the type of inequity society would wish to reduce. The standard deviation and the coefficient of variation attach the same importance to transfers at different payment levels and, therefore, would be inappropriate if society wished to attach more weight to transfers to lower payment levels than higher payment levels. In this instance, it would be more appropriate to use the standard deviation of logarithms since it weights the lower end of the distribution more heavily than the upper end. If, however, society wished to place a heavier weight on the center of the distribution instead of the tails, a Gini coefficient would be a better measure. See Anthony B. Atkinson, "On the Measurement of Inequality," *Journal of Economic Theory*, vol. 2 (1970), pp. 244–63.

TABLE 15

MEASURES OF HORIZONTAL INEQUITY AMONG AGED AND DISABLED
INDIVIDUAL RECIPIENTS, 1973 AND 1976

Measure[a]	Aged[b]		Disabled[c]	
	1973	1976	1973	1976
Recipient rate				
Standard deviation (dollars)	77	68	4.20	7.00
Coefficient of variation	0.92	0.69	0.47	0.46
Standard deviation of logarithms	0.33	0.27	0.22	0.20
Gini coefficient	0.39	0.31	0.24	0.20
Payment standard[d]				
Standard deviation (dollars)	36	30	38	29
Coefficient of variation	0.25	0.16	0.27	0.16
Standard deviation of logarithms	0.11	0.06	0.13	0.06
Average monthly payment per recipient				
Standard deviation (dollars)	15	15	22	21
Coefficient of variation	0.20	0.17	0.22	0.16
Standard deviation of logarithms	0.08	0.07	0.10	0.07
Gini coefficient	0.13	0.12	0.14	0.13
Annual per capita expenditures				
Standard deviation (dollars)	64	72	6	12
Coefficient of variation	0.88	0.71	0.55	0.51
Standard deviation of logarithms	0.33	0.29	0.23	0.22
Gini coefficient	0.41	0.35	0.33	0.26

[a] See text for definitions.

[b] Excludes Alaska, Hawaii, New Hampshire, and Washington, D.C.

[c] Excludes Alaska, Hawaii, Nevada, and Washington, D.C.

[d] Gini coefficients were not calculated because of uncertainty about the number of persons receiving the full standard.

SOURCES: Author's calculations. Methodology discussed in U.S. Bureau of the Census, *Trends in the Income of Families and Persons in the United States, 1947–1964*, Technical Paper 17 (1967), pp. 32–36.

and political pressures to meet special needs. Uniform standards would not allow for special circumstances warranting additional amounts of welfare and would limit a state's ability to tailor assistance to particular needs.

Vertical inequities arise when people in different circumstances are not treated differently—if, for example, a person residing in a Medicaid institution receives the same SSI payment as one living independently or if an SSI recipient whose possessions are destroyed by fire receives the same amount as someone not similarly burdened. Unless a state makes supplementary payments, the recipient usually bears the burden of a fire loss, theft of a check, or other catastrophe.

A major vertical inequity of the SSI program is the exclusion of implicit rent from home ownership in determining SSI eligibility. Also, under current regulations, an otherwise eligible person can own a house of any value and still receive an SSI payment equal to or greater than the amount paid to an SSI recipient who rents an apartment.[17] Vertical inequities also result when individuals with liquid assets equal to the comparable value of a home owned by the typical recipient are denied SSI because of excess resources.

---

[17] To illustrate the concept of imputed income, assume that an individual owns a mortgage-free home with a market value of $40,000. Yearly taxes, insurance, and maintenance are assumed to be 5 percent of the market value of the house, or $2,000 a year. (This figure may be even lower if property taxes are reduced for elderly homeowners.) If the homeowner rented the house at about 10 percent of market value, the imputed net rental income is $2,000 ($4,000 — $2,000). Thus, if the individual did not own the home, he would have had to pay $4,000 to rent it, or $2,000 more than he currently spends for housing. For a discussion, see Federal Council on the Aging, *The Interrelationships of Benefit Programs for the Elderly* (December 29, 1975), pp. 27–28.

3
Raising Persons above Poverty Thresholds

A major objective of the SSI program was to provide the aged, blind, and disabled with a minimum standard of living. As stated by the Senate Committee on Finance, the Social Security Amendments of 1972 "would create a new Federal program . . . designed to provide a positive assurance that the Nation's aged, blind, and disabled people would no longer have to subsist on below-poverty level income."[1]

Two definitions of poverty level income can be used to examine the effect of SSI on the number of persons living in poverty: the poverty thresholds published by the Bureau of the Census and the lower-level budget of the Bureau of Labor Statistics. The Congress probably envisioned the Bureau of the Census figure as the appropriate target. In addition, the success of SSI in reducing poverty can be measured by comparing the incomes of SSI recipients with the incomes of other segments of the population.

Poverty Thresholds

On the basis of work conducted by the Social Security Administration in 1964 and revised by a Federal Interagency Committee in 1969, the Bureau of the Census defines poverty thresholds in terms of the cost of a specific basket of goods and services. A household with less than the poverty threshold is classified as poor; the difference between actual income and threshold income equals the deficit or amount of money the household needs to reach the poverty line. The Social Security Administration has established 124 poverty thresholds, reflecting differences in family size, number of children, age and sex of

---

[1] U.S. Congress, Senate, Committee on Finance, *Social Security Amendments of 1972*, 92nd Congress, 2nd session, September 26, 1972, p. 384.

TABLE 16

Weighted Poverty Thresholds and Annual Federal SSI Payment Standards for Aged Couples and Unrelated Individuals, 1969–1977
(dollars)

	2-Person, Head 65 and Over		Unrelated Individuals, 65 and Over	
Year	Poverty threshold (nonfarm)	Federal SSI standard for the calendar year	Poverty threshold (nonfarm)	Federal SSI standard for the calendar year
1969	2,215	n.a.	1,757	n.a.
1970	2,348	n.a.	1,861	n.a.
1971	2,448	n.a.	1,940	n.a.
1972	2,530	n.a.	2,005	n.a.
1973	2,688	n.a.	2,130	n.a.
1974	2,982	2,574	2,364	1,716
1975	3,257	2,734	2,581	1,822
1976	3,445	2,930	2,730	1,953
1977	3,670[a]	3,110	2,910[a]	2,074

n.a. = Not applicable.

[a] Preliminary estimates.

Sources: U.S. Bureau of the Census, *Current Population Reports*, Series P-60, various issues of "Characteristics of the Low Income Population" and "Money Income of Families and Persons in the United States"; and Table 1 above.

head, and farm or nonfarm residence.[2] "Because it is impractical to use the entire set of 124 poverty lines for anything other than Census surveys or computerized and analytical studies, the Census Bureau publishes the indexes in a simplified form as weighted average cut-offs."[3] Poverty thresholds are updated annually for changes in the consumer price index (CPI). Inflation adjustments, however, may be only approximate because they are not specifically designed for the consumption patterns of poor households.

Table 16 shows the nonfarm poverty thresholds from 1969 to 1977 for unrelated individuals and two-person families whose head is sixty-five years of age or over and the maximum federal SSI pay-

---

[2] The historical development of these thresholds is described in U.S. Department of Health, Education, and Welfare, *The Measure of Poverty* (April 1976), chap. 1.

[3] Ibid., p. 9. For the 124 categories, see p. 10.

ments for 1974 to 1977. In 1977 the thresholds were $2,910 for unrelated individuals and $3,670 for two-person families. The Bureau of the Census defines an aged couple as a household in which one of the two persons is at least sixty-five years of age, and poverty thresholds are based on this definition. On the other hand, the definition of an aged couple on which SSI payments are based is a household in which both persons are at least sixty-five years of age. The welfare needs of an elderly couple both of whom are over sixty-four may be greater than the welfare needs of an elderly couple one of whom is under age sixty-five. If so, to achieve the same standard of living, SSI payments would have to be larger than the poverty threshold. The comparisons of SSI payments and the Census Bureau poverty thresholds in this chapter do not make allowances for this possibility; rather, it is assumed that there is only a small difference in the needs of elderly couples regardless of whether both partners are over sixty-four.

BLS Budgets

Each year, the Bureau of Labor Statistics (BLS) publishes three budgets indicating the amount of income an urban household needs for different living levels—lower, intermediate, and higher.[4] These budgets are calculated for both four-person urban families and retired couples.[5] Equivalency scales are used to estimate budgets for other household sizes. Separate budgets are calculated for forty metropolitan areas and four nonmetropolitan regions, and area differences in living requirements and tastes are taken into account. The budgets are adjusted annually for price changes of major classes of goods and services.[6]

Lower-level BLS consumption budgets for aged units are shown

---

[4] Data sources, methods of calculation, and goods and services in the budgets can be found in Bureau of Labor Statistics, *Three Standards of Living for the Urban Family of Four Persons*, Spring 1967, Bulletin 1570-5 (1969).

[5] In the four-person family, a thirty-eight-year-old husband employed full time has a nonworking wife, a boy of thirteen, and a girl of eight. It is assumed that the couple has been married about fifteen years, that the family is settled in the community, and that the husband is an experienced worker. At each budget level, the family has an average stock of clothing, house furnishings, major durables, and other equipment. A retired couple is a husband aged sixty-five or over and his wife. They are self-supporting, reside in an urban area, are in reasonably good health, and are able to take care of themselves.

[6] The last direct pricing occurred in 1969. Findings of the 1972–1973 Consumer Expenditure Survey will yield new information on actual spending patterns. For a description of the survey, see Michael D. Carlson, "The 1972–73 Consumer Expenditure Survey," *Monthly Labor Review*, vol. 97 (December 1974), pp. 16–23.

TABLE 17

LOWER-LEVEL BLS CONSUMPTION BUDGETS, SELECTED AGED UNITS,
1973–1977
(dollars)

Year	Single Persons, 65 and Over	Husband and Wife, 65 and Over	Retired Couples
1973	1,840	3,360	3,763
1974	2,050	3,730	4,228
1975	2,180	3,980	4,308
1976	2,290	4,160	4,493
1977	2,420	4,410	4,815

NOTE: Autumn of each year. The budgets for retired couples are based on an independent pricing of various goods and services. The budgets for aged couples are obtained by applying an equivalency scale to the budgets for a four-person family.

SOURCES: Bureau of Labor Statistics, various issues of *Monthly Labor Review* and *Autumn Family Budgets and Comparative Indexes for Selected Urban Areas.*

in Table 17.[7] The budgets for aged individuals and aged couples are obtained by use of equivalency scales: the budget for a four-person family is multiplied by 0.28 for individuals and by 0.51 for aged couples. The budgets for retired couples are estimated independently rather than based on an equivalency scale. The BLS budgets do not suggest how income should be spent, however, nor are they specifically intended to measure the amount of income necessary for poverty-level subsistence. Rather, they show the amount of income required for three styles of living and, unlike the Social Security Administration's thresholds, they are not constructed around the notion of providing adequate nutrition.[8]

In the autumn of 1977 the lower-level budget for an aged single person was $2,420 compared with $4,410 for an aged couple. A comparison of the Social Security Administration's thresholds with the

---

[7] Consumption budgets exclude: (1) allowances for gifts and contributions, life insurance, and occupational expenses; and (2) social security and disability payments, and personal income taxes. These items can be ignored when analyzing payment standards for persons with no countable income since only a small amount of money would be needed for these purposes. The 1977 lower budget for a four-person family included $1,352 for taxes and $472 for other items.

[8] In general, the Social Security Administration's thresholds are a multiple of the amount of income that the government defines as necessary to purchase an adequate level of nutrition. On the difficulty of estimating the cost of food needs, see George J. Stigler, "The Cost of Subsistence," *Journal of Farm Economics*, vol. 27 (May 1945), pp. 303–14.

lower-level BLS budgets shows that in 1977 the threshold for aged individuals was about 20 percent higher than the corresponding lower-level BLS budget. The BLS budget for aged couples, however, was about 20 percent higher than its poverty threshold counterpart. The BLS budget for a retired couple was 30 percent greater than the Social Security Administration benchmark.

Relative Thresholds. Absolute income thresholds reflect one dimension of economic life—the ability to purchase a bundle of commodities. Yet a household's economic status, self-perception of its well-being, and ability to partake in mainstream sociopolitical activities depend not only on its absolute level of income but also on its income relative to that of other households.[9] Estimates of relative poverty may be made by counting as poor every person falling below the median income or below a specific proportion of the income distribution, such as the lowest quintile or quartile. With a relative definition, it is more difficult for society to eliminate poverty because the poverty gap increases annually in response to real improvements in living standards as well as price increases.

Poverty among the Elderly. Figure 1 shows that poverty among the elderly declined principally before SSI was established in 1974. In 1967 elderly persons were more than twice as likely as the rest of the nation to be poor—29.5 percent of the elderly (5.4 million persons) had incomes below poverty thresholds in that year, as compared with 12.6 percent of the nonelderly persons. The situation has changed dramatically since the Congress has granted comparatively substantial increases in social security benefits and the states have provided the needy with additional welfare payments.[10] In 1974, 15.7 percent

---

[9] Research suggests that, as their own economic circumstances improve, taxpayers individually raise the poverty threshold by an amount that is proportionately less than the increase in their own income. See Larry L. Orr, "Income Transfers as a Public Good: An Application to AFDC," *American Economic Review*, vol. 66 (June 1976), pp. 367–68; and Robert W. Kilpatrick, "The Income Elasticity of the Poverty Line," *Review of Economics and Statistics*, vol. 55 (August 1973), pp. 327–32.

[10] The proportion of poverty income to median income for two-person families with an aged head and unrelated aged individuals declined between 1969 and 1976. Although the figures are not strictly comparable because of recent methodological revisions, the proportion for the former fell from 52 to 42.8 percent and for the latter from 94.7 to 78.1 percent. Hence, if a household in either cohort had an annual income equal to the poverty threshold, it would have experienced increasing relative deprivation over these years. The additional deprivation was about the same for both aged units, with most of the decline occurring between 1969 and 1973. Thereafter, the relative threshold was a fairly constant proportion of median income, but lower than the threshold in 1969.

FIGURE 1

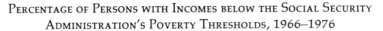

PERCENTAGE OF PERSONS WITH INCOMES BELOW THE SOCIAL SECURITY
ADMINISTRATION'S POVERTY THRESHOLDS, 1966–1976

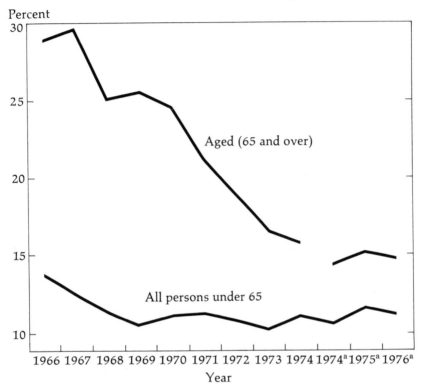

Year

[a] Revised methodology; data not strictly comparable with other years. The break
shows the beginning of the revised series.

SOURCE: U.S. Bureau of the Census, *Current Population Reports*, "Money Income
and Poverty Status of Persons in the United States," Advance Report, Series
P-60, no. 107 (1977), table 16.

of the aged (3.3 million persons) were poor, as compared with about
11 percent of the remainder of the population. Figure 2 shows that
the proportion of poor persons who were aged fell from 19.4 percent
in 1967 to 13.6 percent in 1974.

The downward trend in poverty among the elderly was actually
interrupted in 1975 and 1976 after SSI was established. The number
of poor aged persons climbed by 7.6 percent between 1974 and 1976
in contrast with 6.8 percent for persons below age sixty-five. The
faster growth in the incidence of poverty among the elderly, however,
was accompanied by an opposite change in the number of persons

FIGURE 2

The Aged Poor as a Percentage of All Poor Persons, 1966–1976

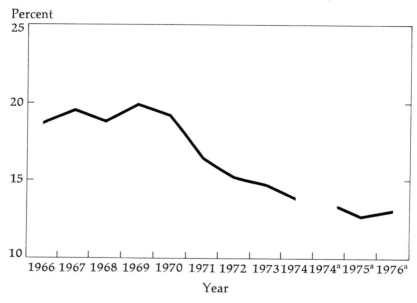

^a Revised methodology; data not strictly comparable with other years. The break
shows the beginning of the revised series.

Source: U.S. Bureau of the Census, *Current Population Reports*, "Money Income
and Poverty Status," table 16.

with incomes below 75 percent of the poverty threshold—the number
of aged persons below this benchmark rose by 5.8 percent, as compared with 6.4 percent for the nonaged.[11] Hence, contrary to past
experiences, the aged may not have borne a disproportionate share of
the hardships resulting from the 1974–1976 increase in the poverty
count.

SSI Payment Standards and Poverty Thresholds

As Table 16 shows, in calendar year 1974 eligible aged individuals
received a maximum federal SSI income of $1,716; eligible aged
couples received $2,574. The 1974 poverty thresholds were $2,364 for
aged individuals and $2,982 for aged couples; the lower-level BLS
budgets shown in Table 17 totaled $2,050 for individuals and $3,730
for a husband and wife, sixty-five and over. The federal payment

---

[11] Based on unpublished data furnished by the Bureau of the Census.

standard alone did not raise persons with no other income to either the poverty thresholds or to the lower-level BLS budgets.[12] The federal standards were also less than the thresholds and budgets from 1975 to 1977.

The SSI program has done more to eliminate poverty for some recipients than for others. In July 1977 the federal standards comprised a higher proportion of the poverty lines for residents of rural areas than for those in urban areas and represented a larger fraction of the threshold for aged couples than for individuals. Aged urban couples could secure 85 percent of the poverty level, as compared with 71 percent for individuals because the SSI standard for couples was 50 percent higher than for individuals, whereas poverty thresholds for individuals and couples differed by only 26 percent. Conversely, the SSI program helped aged individuals meet 88 percent of their BLS equivalency budget needs, as compared with 73 percent for couples (66 percent for retired couples).

State supplements raised the income of eligible persons closer to the poverty line. In 1977 thirteen states had supplementary standards for basic needs of aged couples that raised the combined standard to at least the national threshold for nonfarm areas.[13] About 30 percent of all SSI aged couples with a federally administered payment in 1977 resided in these states. Similarly, the combined standards in six states abolished poverty for aged individuals in nonfarm areas; approximately 20 percent of all individual SSI recipients resided in these states.[14] As for the income shortfall of the remaining recipients, the economic hardships were at least partly alleviated by Medicaid, food stamps, and housing allowances.

Table 18 shows for selected states the ratio of the combined federal-state payment standards to the poverty threshold for aged persons residing in nonfarm areas. An increasing ratio means that the standard increased at a faster rate than the poverty threshold. In 1973 these states, except for Mississippi, guaranteed eligible aged residents income that was at least 90 percent of the national benchmark. From 1973 to 1974 ratios increased substantially in four of the six states, especially in Mississippi. Over the next three years, however, all of the ratios declined, some by comparatively large amounts. These declines are largely attributable to states not passing along the

---

[12] The Senate bill proposed standards of $130 and $195 at a time when the thresholds were $167 and $211.

[13] Alaska, California, Colorado, Connecticut, Massachusetts, Nebraska, Nevada, New York, Oklahoma, Pennsylvania, Rhode Island, Vermont, and Wisconsin.

[14] Alaska, California, Connecticut, Massachusetts, Nebraska, and Wisconsin.

TABLE 18

RATIO OF PAYMENT STANDARDS TO POVERTY THRESHOLDS FOR AGED
INDIVIDUALS AND COUPLES, SELECTED STATES AND YEARS

State	1973[a]		1974[b]		1977[b]	
	Indi-viduals	Couples	Indi-viduals	Couples	Indi-viduals	Couples
United States	—[c]	—[c]	0.73	0.86	0.71	0.85
California	1.13	1.63	1.19	1.77	1.18	1.76
Illinois	0.96	0.96	0.89	0.88	0.74	0.85
Mississippi	0.42	0.67	0.73	0.86	0.71	0.85
New Jersey	0.91	0.99	0.92	1.01	0.80	0.88
New York	0.95	1.08	1.05	1.19	0.96	1.10
Wisconsin	1.13	1.09	1.13[d]	1.35[d]	1.01	1.20

NOTE: Table refers to nonfarm residents only.
[a] July 1, 1973.
[b] Ratios based on standards in effect on January 1 and July 1.
[c] No national standard.
[d] Includes retroactive adjustment implemented in 1975.
SOURCES. Author's calculations. Payment standards from Table 2; poverty thresholds from U.S. Bureau of the Census, *Current Population Reports*, "Characteristics of the Low Income Population," Series P-60.

total cost-of-living increases in federal standards and/or to states not fully price-adjusting their supplementary standards for local inflation.

Differences in the real incomes of recipients may not be as large as the ratios in Table 18 suggest because payments are not adjusted for interstate variations in price levels. Although price indexes for each state are unavailable, price indexes for metropolitan areas are published regularly. Table 19 shows the real change in standards for aged persons residing in selected areas from January 1974 to July 1977, and from July 1973 to July 1977, using the different price indexes for metropolitan areas. The later period shows the change from the six-month period before SSI was implemented to 1977. The July 1973 standard represents the largest amount a state paid to an elderly woman (no information available for males). It was assumed that women residing in metropolitan areas would be more likely to receive this payment than those in rural areas because urban areas ordinarily experience higher living costs.

For the United States as a whole, aged recipients with only a federal payment averaged 2.7 percent ($3.81) less in purchasing power in July 1977 than January 1974 because of a time lag in the cost-of-living adjustment. Except for a nominal gain in New York (including northeastern New Jersey), the real loss varied from $0.06 in Chicago to $10.73 in Houston. In Boston, Philadelphia, and Pittsburgh, the real loss in federal payments was outweighed by real increases in state supplementary standards. In other areas, however, the loss in federal payments was not offset (or was magnified by a decline in the real value of supplementation)—once again largely because the state did not pass along the full cost-of-living increase in the federal standard and/or did not fully price-adjust its supplementary standards to counter local price increases. As a result, many SSI recipients had less real welfare income in July 1977 than they did when SSI began.

A different picture emerges when the real value of the standards in July 1973 is compared with the real value in July 1977: real gains were realized in most metropolitan areas. These gains are largely attributable to the rise in standards that occurred with the advent of SSI. Data for 1974 and 1977 suggest, however, that these gains could erode over time if prices increase faster and the cost-of-living lag is not reduced, and state supplementary standards do not keep pace with inflation.[15]

SSI Payment Standards and BLS Budgets. The effect of SSI on raising incomes of low-income aged persons may also be shown by changes in the ratio of SSI standards to lower-level BLS budgets. Since both the SSI standards and the BLS budgets are adjusted annually for inflation, an increase in this ratio would indicate a rise in real income. Since the goods and services constituting a level vary from one area to another, however, a higher ratio of SSI payments to the BLS lower-level budget in one area does not necessarily mean that persons in that area were better off than persons elsewhere.[16]

These ratios for selected metropolitan areas are reported in Table 20. Changes in them resemble changes in Table 19 insofar as large increases occurred after the advent of the SSI program, and the ratios

---

[15] A relative definition of poverty suggests that SSI helped to halt the decline in relative deprivation but did not restore the poverty line to its position in 1969.

[16] Area comparisons implicitly assume that residents of one place would be equally satisfied with items consumed in other areas. This may not be so. To illustrate, pork and lard are weighted heavier in budgets for the South than the Northeast, whereas larger weights are assigned to beef and butter in the Northeast than the South. Residents in one area, therefore, may not be equally satisfied with the commodities consumed in other areas. For a discussion of this and other problems, see U.S. Department of Health, Education, and Welfare, *The Measure of Poverty*, Technical Paper IV: "Bureau of Labor Statistics Family Budgets Program," pp. 10–13.

TABLE 19

CHANGE IN THE REAL VALUE OF THE PAYMENT STANDARD FOR THE BASIC NEEDS OF INDIVIDUALS LIVING INDEPENDENTLY AND HAVING NO COUNTABLE INCOME, SIXTEEN AREAS, 1973–1977

Area	January 1974–July 1977				July 1973–July 1977 Federal-State Standard	
	Federal standard		Federal-state standard			
	Amount (dollars)	Percent	Amount (dollars)	Percent	Amount (dollars)	Percent
United States	− 3.81	−2.7	− 3.81[a]	− 2.7[a]	—[b]	—[b]
Northeast						
Boston	− 3.39	−2.4	4.94	2.2	11.22	5.5
New York–Northeast New Jersey[c]						
New York	0.16	0.1	−18.81	− 9.1	10.36	6.2
New Jersey	0.16	0.1	−24.52	−13.5	−12.75	− 7.9
Philadelphia	− 2.44	−1.7	12.29	8.2	7.17	4.9
Pittsburgh	− 2.65	−1.9	12.04	8.0	8.19	5.6
North Central						
Chicago	− 0.06	−0.1	−29.56	−16.9	−33.15	−19.4
Cleveland[a]	− 0.28	−0.2	− 0.28	− 0.2	2.53	1.9
Milwaukee[d]	− 1.59	−1.1	−18.49	− 8.6	−11.73	− 5.8
St. Louis[d]	− 5.76	−4.1	− 5.76	− 4.1	43.51	51.2

South						
Atlanta[d]	− 1.91	−1.4	− 1.91	− 1.4	32.75	33.1
Baltimore[d]	− 5.25	−3.8	− 5.25	− 3.8	31.97	33.3
Dallas[d]	− 3.81	−2.7	− 3.81	− 2.7	7.50	6.1
Houston	−10.73	−7.7	−10.73	− 7.7	− 0.83	− 0.7
West						
Los Angeles–Long Beach	− 6.57	−4.7	−13.11	− 5.6	11.88	5.9
San Diego	− 4.43	−3.2	− 9.56	− 4.1	16.06	8.0
San Francisco–Oakland	− 6.87	−4.9	−13.61	− 5.8	14.03	7.0
Seattle	− 5.86	−4.2	− 5.72[e]	− 3.4[e]	− 3.17[e]	− 2.0[e]

[a] Federal standard only. Standards rounded to the nearest dollar.
[b] No national standard.
[c] Applies to appropriate parts of these states.
[d] Price indexes for months closest to the study periods.
[e] Area I.

SOURCES: Author's calculations. Payment standards from Appendix, Table A-1; price indexes from Bureau of Labor Statistics, *Consumer Price Index*, various issues.

either decreased or increased by a smaller amount between 1974 and 1977 than between 1973 and 1974. In contrast with the real declines shown in Table 19, SSI recipients in southern areas were generally better able to purchase the baskets in 1977 than in 1974, even though their real SSI incomes fell over this period. One possible explanation for these seemingly inconsistent findings is that the baskets of goods and services making up the budgets are price adjusted by components, whereas SSI standards are adjusted annually by the change in the entire CPI. As a result, if the CPI rises at a faster rate than the cost of a budget basket, a recipient may be wealthier in terms of the basket but poorer in terms of CPI-based real income. Another possible explanation is that the data in Tables 19 and 20 are centered at different points in time; a third is that the use of the same equivalency scales across areas may not have been entirely appropriate.

Poverty Gaps. The ratios in Tables 19 and 20 and the data in Tables 13 and 14 are for recipients with no countable income and do not show the impact of SSI on recipients in other financial circumstances. It is possible, therefore, that not all SSI payments were received by poor persons. Instead, they might have gone to recipients whose pre-SSI income was above the poverty threshold or to persons who continued to receive SSI after their total income reached the poverty line.

The success of SSI in helping persons with different financial needs can be estimated by examining changes in the poverty ratio— the ratio of the actual income a household receives to the poverty threshold. Given nonwelfare income, an increase in a ratio that is initially less than one would signify a reduction in poverty.[17]

Initial findings of the Social Security Administration's Survey of Low-Income Aged and Disabled (SLIAD) persons show that the SSI program has had a substantial effect on relieving poverty among noninstitutionalized, grandfathered, aged, blind, and disabled recipients.[18] Between 1973 and 1974 the poverty ratio increased for about

---

[17] The poverty ratio does not allow for variations in need. Economic theory suggests that income transfers should be weighted by need since poorer households probably value a specific transfer more than less needy households. For alternative approaches, see Marilyn Moon, *The Measurement of Economic Welfare: Its Application to the Aged Poor* (New York: Academic Press, 1977), chaps. 3 and 4.

[18] For a discussion of this survey, see Thomas Tissue, "Survey of the Low-Income Aged and Disabled," *Social Security Bulletin*, vol. 40 (February 1977), pp. 3–11. It is probably true that for many SSI recipients there was little or no correlation between welfare gains and perception of well being. For information about the 1973 welfare population, see Social Security Administration, *Survey of Low-Income Aged and Disabled: A Last Look at Adult Welfare Recipients Prior to SSI*, Report no. 3 (1978), pp. 25–27.

two-thirds of these recipients.[19] Almost 30 percent reported a gain of 0.10 to 0.24, while another one-third gained up to 0.10.[20] Much of the gain was realized by the poorest families. Of the 10 percent of the aged persons with a 1973 poverty ratio lower than 0.50, about 83 percent had a higher ratio in 1974. The comparable figure for one-quarter of the blind and disabled with poverty incomes in 1973 was 78 percent. Similarly, many recipients with a 1973 poverty ratio in excess of 0.75—including recipients whose 1973 ratio was in excess of 1.25—reported a higher ratio in 1974.[21]

The success of SSI in abolishing poverty can also be evaluated in absolute terms by analyzing the program's effect on the poverty gap—the difference between actual income and the Social Security Administration's poverty threshold. If SSI has been successful in eradicating poverty, the post-SSI gap would be smaller than the pre-SSI gap. The proportion of the reduction in poverty attributable to SSI can be measured by dividing the difference in the gaps by the SSI payments. This proportion is expressed by the following formula:

$$PR = \frac{A - B}{S},$$

where PR = proportion of SSI payments that closed the pre-SSI poverty gap, A = pre-SSI poverty gap, B = post-SSI poverty gap, and S = SSI payments. If PR is 0.80, four-fifths of the SSI payments would have been used to reduce the pre-SSI poverty gap. If $A = B$, none of the payments would have gone to poor households. But if $B = 0$, or if $A = S$, SSI could be credited with abolishing poverty among the targeted groups.

The pre-SSI poverty gap in 1974 was $2.1 billion for the aged and $2.2 billion for the blind and disabled. In 1974 the SSI program closed about 72 percent of the gap for each recipient group; the 1973 programs closed only 61 percent of that year's gap. SSI was also more successful than previous programs in raising people above poverty thresholds. About one-quarter of each group was lifted out of poverty in 1974, as compared with 25.5 percent of the aged and 18.1 percent of the disabled in the previous year.

---

[19] The SLIAD shows that nonassistance income kept pace with rising prices. Hence, an improvement in a poverty ratio would be associated with the SSI program.

[20] Sylvester J. Schieber, "First-Year Impact of SSI on Economic Status of 1973 Adult Assistance Populations," *Social Security Bulletin*, vol. 41 (February 1978), pp. 1–29.

[21] Ibid., table 14.

TABLE 20

RATIO OF PUBLIC ASSISTANCE AND SSI STANDARDS TO BLS LOWER-LEVEL CONSUMPTION BUDGETS FOR AGED INDIVIDUALS AND COUPLES, SIXTEEN AREAS, 1973, 1974, AND 1977

Area	1973		1974		1977	
	Individuals	Couples	Individuals	Couples	Individuals	Couples
United States	—[a]	—[a]	0.85[b]	0.70[b]	0.88[b]	0.73[b]
Northeast						
Boston	1.24	1.01	1.49	1.25	1.38	1.15
New York–Northeast New Jersey[c]						
New York	1.04	0.82	1.14	0.90	1.13	0.89
New Jersey	1.01	0.76	1.01	0.76	0.95	0.72
Philadelphia–New Jersey[d]	0.96	0.79	1.00	0.83	1.04	0.85
Pittsburgh	0.99	0.81	1.02	0.84	1.08	0.89
North Central						
Cedar Rapids	0.85	0.72	0.88	0.73	0.91	0.75
Champaign–Urbana	1.06	0.73	0.99	0.68	0.88	0.70
Dayton	0.89	0.83	0.89	0.73	0.93	0.77
Milwaukee	1.34	0.89	1.27	1.07	1.27	1.06
South						
Atlanta	0.67	0.62	0.90	0.74	0.94	0.77
Baton Rouge	0.76	0.79	0.92	0.76	0.94	0.77

Houston	0.85	0.76	0.90	0.74	0.90	0.74
Nashville	0.67	0.65	0.91	0.75	0.95	0.78
West						
Bakersfield	1.34	1.34	1.43	1.47	1.49	1.54
Denver	0.99	1.08	1.03	1.12	1.09	1.19
Los Angeles–Long Beach	1.25	1.25	1.32	1.36	1.38	1.43
San Francisco–Oakland	1.20	1.19	1.27	1.30	1.34	1.38

a No national standard.
b Federal payment only. Standards rounded to the nearest dollar.
c Applies to appropriate parts of these states.
d Based on standards in Pennsylvania.

SOURCES: Author's calculations. Payment standards from Social Security Administration, *Supplemental Security Income for the Aged, Blind, and Disabled: Summary of State Payment Levels, State Supplementation, and Medicaid Decisions*; budgets from Bureau of Labor Statistics, *Monthly Labor Review*, various issues.

TABLE 21

Percentage Distribution of Aged, Blind, and Disabled Public Assistance and SSI Recipients, by Poverty Ratio, 1973 and 1974

Poverty Ratio	Aged Recipients		Blind and Disabled Recipients	
	1973	1974	1973	1974
0–0.24	0.6	0.3	3.4	0.9
0.25–0.49	9.8	3.3	21.9	7.6
0.50–0.74	33.7	25.3	28.8	35.2
0.75–0.99	24.7	39.0	23.2	24.8
1.00–1.24	17.3	16.2	13.1	17.8
1.25–1.99	12.8	14.9	7.9	11.2
2.00 and above	1.1	1.1	1.8	2.7
All persons	100.0	100.0	100.0	100.0
Persons reporting (thousands)	1,619.7	1,459.7	1,125.0	1,055.9

Note: Detail may not add to the total because of rounding.

Source: Sylvester J. Schieber, "First-Year Impact of SSI on Economic Status of 1973 Adult Assistance Populations," *Social Security Bulletin*, vol. 41 (February 1978), tables 5 and 8.

Table 21 shows that, even with the improvement in the poverty ratios and the reduction in the poverty gap, most grandfathered recipients were still poor in 1974. A sizable number of them had a ratio between 0.75 and 1.00, suggesting that a relatively nominal increase in standards would lift many of these individuals out of poverty. Nonetheless, more than a few recipients still had a ratio below 0.50 in 1974.

According to Table 22, SSI's effectiveness in closing poverty gaps varied by state. For example, half the payments to the aged in California and 30 percent of the payments to their blind and disabled peers did not close poverty gaps, as compared with less than 7 percent of the payments in Texas and Georgia. It would seem, therefore, that more poverty according to the Social Security Administration's thresholds could be eliminated if fewer SSI funds were spent in California than in other states.

Perhaps the most surprising information shown in Table 22 is that, in certain instances, SSI lifted a relatively smaller number of persons above the poverty threshold than did the previous programs. In Mississippi, for example, 1973 welfare payments raised about 20 percent of pre-assistance aged poor persons above the poverty threshold, as compared with 12 percent for SSI payments. Nevertheless, in Mississippi and the other states, SSI closed a larger portion of the poverty gap than did the previous programs.

Several factors explain why SSI did not lift more people out of poverty. In some states the rate of increase in payment standards was less than the rate of increase in poverty thresholds. In other states the increase in payment levels was greater than the increase in thresholds but was still insufficient to bring recipients up to the poverty benchmark. For some recipients the increase in assistance income was less than the decline in other income. Also, some recipients experienced welfare-related harmful changes in their living arrangements or other characteristics, and some recipients were hurt by adverse interrelationships between the old and the new programs.

Effects of SSI When In-Kind Income Is Included

The exclusion of in-kind income significantly understates the gross income of low-income households and overstates the number of poor people.[22] A decade ago Medicare and Medicaid were in their infancy, and less than $40 million was spent on food stamps and housing assistance; in 1976, however, the national bill for in-kind transfers for Medicaid, Medicare, and food stamps reached $35 billion, with an estimated 6.8 million aged, blind, and disabled persons receiving Medicaid services alone. A recent study by the Department of Health, Education, and Welfare concludes: "Empirical evidence for 1974 and several earlier years indicates that if food stamps were included as income and if the poverty thresholds were not changed, about 5 to 15 percent of the poor (depending on the method of valuation used) would no longer be counted as poor."[23]

It is difficult to estimate the value of in-kind benefits. A dollar of in-kind income may not be worth as much as a dollar of cash income because of differences in a recipient's ability to express tastes and preferences.[24] Inclusion of in-kind income also introduces questions about the need to adjust poverty thresholds accordingly. In any event, in-kind transfers do augment income and must be counted in

---

[22] In-kind transfers consist primarily of child nutrition, food stamps, housing assistance, Medicare, and Medicaid.

[23] U.S. Department of Health, Education, and Welfare, *The Measure of Poverty*, pp. xxiv–xxv.

[24] Clarkson estimates that recipients value food stamps at four-fifths their market value (face minus purchase price). See Kenneth W. Clarkson, *Food Stamps and Nutrition* (Washington, D.C.: American Enterprise Institute, 1975).

TABLE 22

The Reduction in Poverty among Aged, Blind, and Disabled Public Assistance and SSI Recipients, 1973 and 1974

	United States		California	
Measure	1973	1974	1973	1974
Aged recipients				
Percentage of poor recipients				
Pre-public assistance	92.3	91.0	75.2	77.8
Post-public assistance	68.8	67.8	12.2	7.8
Percentage of the poverty gap eliminated				
by public assistance	61.9	72.8	94.9	95.7
Percentage of payments that closed				
poverty gap	81.4	82.5	52.3	50.4
Blind and disabled recipients				
Percentage of poor recipients				
Pre-public assistance	94.3	92.9	84.7	85.3
Post-public assistance	77.2	67.3	40.4	14.6
Percentage of poverty gap eliminated by				
public assistance	60.2	71.3	87.8	96.2
Percentage of payments that closed				
poverty gap	87.8	86.7	75.0	70.5

Source: Schieber, "First-Year Impact of SSI on Economic Status of 1973 Adult Assistance Populations," tables 5, 8, 16, and 20; and unpublished data provided by Sylvester J. Schieber.

order to portray accurately the economic status of low-income persons.

In-kind and money transfer programs may interact in two ways. First, eligibility for one program may affect eligibility for another. In July 1977, for example, SSI recipients were automatically eligible for food stamps in most states, while two-thirds of the states automatically entitled all SSI recipients to Medicaid services. Newly entitled welfare recipients averaged large gains in in-kind transfers because Medicaid eligibility is an all-or-nothing proposition; there is no sliding scale by level of income. Second, the dollar value of benefits received from one program may reduce the benefits available from another program. For example, an increase in SSI income usually reduces the bonus value of food stamps since the cost of the stamps varies directly with an individual's ability to pay for them. Least likely to have realized additional in-kind income are grandfathered recipients who resided in states with relatively generous pre-SSI in-kind programs.

Georgia		Mississippi		New York		Texas		Other States	
1973	1974	1973	1974	1973	1974	1973	1974	1973	1974
94.9	95.8	97.2	97.6	92.2	92.5	97.9	97.6	95.3	95.3
86.5	82.5	77.3	85.5	51.1	36.3	93.9	87.5	78.8	79.2
51.1	69.6	53.2	67.1	78.6	86.4	50.5	66.1	59.6	70.2
93.5	94.4	91.4	94.2	80.7	78.1	96.2	97.1	89.1	90.3
94.4	96.5	96.2	96.8	96.1	95.1	97.1	95.0	96.4	94.2
89.5	87.5	89.8	90.9	72.1	62.2	93.4	90.4	86.9	81.9
45.3	60.0	41.7	56.6	74.3	84.1	46.4	55.8	53.5	65.0
94.1	94.0	95.3	94.7	88.9	88.3	95.4	93.9	93.4	92.4

Estimates based on a microsimulated model developed by the Urban Institute indicate that 97 percent of SSI households with a federally administered payment in 1975 participated in the food stamp or Medicaid programs.[25] Almost 55 percent received both Medicaid and SSI, 3 percent received SSI and food stamps, and 39 percent participated in all three programs, with the typical newly awarded SSI recipient averaging $339 in Medicaid benefits. Because

[25] The model analyzes interactions between SSI, Medicaid, and food stamps for households whose head was sixty years and over. Essentially, the model consists of modules that represent mathematical formulations of the rules and regulations of tax and transfer programs. Circumstances for individual households are captured by the model to determine whether the unit is entitled to a benefit, the amount of the benefit, and whether the unit actually participates in a program. For additional details, see the Federal Council on Aging, *The Interrelationships of Benefit Programs for the Elderly*, Appendix III: "The Combined Impact of Selected Benefit Programs on Older Americans: A Trim Analysis" (December 29, 1975).

of the magnitude of in-kind transfers, poverty may not be as pervasive as some official statistics indicate.[26] A recent study by the Congressional Budget Office estimates that in fiscal 1976 in-kind transfers reduced the proportion of poor households with an aged head (after cash transfers but before taxes) from 16.7 percent of the total to 6.1 percent.[27]

---

[26] This suggestion parallels the findings with respect to the national population in Edgar K. Browning, "How Much More Equality Can We Afford?" *Public Interest*, no. 43 (Spring 1976), pp. 90–110.

[27] Congressional Budget Office, *Poverty Status of Families under Alternative Definitions of Income* (June 1977), p. 31. The 6.1 percent rises to 14 percent if Medicare and Medicaid are excluded from the analysis. One reason for excluding them is to avoid the implication that poor persons could rise out of poverty by becoming seriously ill, such as by contracting kidney disease or requiring institutionalization for mental disease.

During the first quarter of 1976, about 11 percent of the SSI recipients also received social services under Title XX of the Social Security Act, ranging from less than 1 percent in Arizona and Indiana to almost 29 percent in Maryland. See Social Security Administration, "SSI Recipients Receiving Social Services, January-March 1976," *Research and Statistics Note*, note 1 (January 26, 1978), table 7.

4

Impact of SSI on Welfare Payments by State Governments

A major political attraction of the SSI program was the expectation that it would provide state governments with fiscal relief from mounting welfare costs. This chapter analyzes the success of the SSI program in achieving this goal, its impact on the distribution of federal welfare dollars among states, and its impact on the cost of state Medicaid programs.

Pre-SSI Matching Arrangements

In 1973 the cost of welfare programs for the aged, blind, and disabled was shared by the federal and state governments.[1] Federal law permitted the states to calculate the federal share of assistance payments in either of two ways. First, a state could elect to have the federal government pay 31/37 of the first $37 of a recipient's monthly payment plus the state's federal welfare match for payments between $37 and $75. Amounts exceeding $75 were the state's responsibility.[2] Second, a state with a Medicaid program could apply its federal match for Medicaid payments against welfare payments, without any ceiling on the federal share.[3] Both the Medicaid and the federal welfare

---

[1] The state share was partly funded by lower levels of government. Throughout the chapter, the state share includes the local share of the payments.

[2] The federal percentage (F) for the ith state for amounts between $37 and $75 was determined as follows:

$$F_i = 1.00 - 0.50 \frac{Y_i^2}{Y_n^2}, \text{ with } 0.50 \leq F_i \leq 0.65, \text{ and where } Y_i = \text{state per}$$

capita income and Y_n = national per capita income.

[3] The Federal percentage for Medicaid payments was determined in the following manner:

$$F_i = 1.00 - 0.45 \frac{Y_i^2}{Y_n^2}, \text{ with } 0.50 \leq F_i \leq 0.83.$$

61

matches were inversely related to state per capita income. Since wealthy states usually had comparatively high welfare payment standards, they typically chose the Medicaid match because of the absence of a ceiling on federally matched welfare payments. Poorer states were often able to maximize federal financial participation by using the other method.

The state share of welfare payments for the aged, blind, and disabled increased from $1.0 billion in fiscal year 1970 to $1.3 billion in 1973.[4] Part of this increase resulted from an increase in the number of recipients, another part from increases in payment standards. The percentage increase varied markedly among states. For example, state welfare payments increased 49 percent in Massachusetts and 98 percent in New York, as compared with 13 percent in California and 1.7 percent in Oklahoma. In a few states, payments actually declined between 1970 and 1973.

Arrangements under SSI

The federal government absorbs the entire cost of the federal SSI payments. Although state governments finance the bulk of the supplementary payments, under certain circumstances the federal government pays a portion of them. Initially, the federal government agreed to pay part of a state's supplementary payments if the state elected to have the federal government administer its supplementary payments and if the combined federal-state SSI payment standard did not exceed the state's adjusted payment level (APL)—the average amount paid to recipients in January 1972.[5] If the state fulfilled these

---

[4] U.S. Department of Health, Education, and Welfare, *State Expenditures for Public Assistance Programs Approved under Titles I, IV-A, X, XIV, and XIX of the Social Security Act*, reports for fiscal years 1970 and 1973 (1971 and 1974).

[5] The enabling legislation defined the APL as the average amount plus, at state option, the sum of a payment level modification and the bonus value of food stamps, which was $10 per recipient per month. The payment level modification was to affect states that paid less than their 1972 standard of need. These states were to be permitted to raise their January 1972 payment level by a fraction of the difference between the maximum allowable payment for basic needs and the standard of need without loss of financial protection for the incremental amount. As it turned out, the bonus value and payment level modification played a nominal role in the development of the APL.

The APL has, however, proved extremely difficult to calculate. California, New York, and Wisconsin have each disputed its APL as estimated by the HEW Audit Agency. Each felt the estimate was low and contested its financial liability for a portion of the supplementary payments made in its behalf. In support of their position, California and New York withheld $37 million in reimbursements for supplementary payments in 1974 and $84 million in 1975. See U.S. Congress, House of Representatives, Subcommittee on Public Assistance of the Committee on Ways and Means, *Supplemental Security Income Program*, vol. 1, 94th Congress, 1st session, June 3, 1975, p. 29.

requirements, its aggregate supplementation costs were to be limited to the amount the state paid in 1972 to aged, blind, and disabled persons.

To illustrate, assume that the average payment level was $162 in 1972 and that it was shared equally by the federal and state governments—a cost to each of $81. In January 1974 the state had to make an average payment to an individual of only $22—the federal SSI standard was $140 (see Table 2). If SSI had not increased the number of welfare recipients and if the state did not increase its standard above $162, the state would have reduced its spending in 1974 by $59 ($81 — $22) a person. If the number of recipients increased and if each of them received a supplement of $22, total state spending would be limited to total 1972 payments because of the hold-harmless provision (see below). Hence, the states were protected against fiscal problems caused by SSI's loosening of eligibility criteria for welfare. If the state paid a supplement greater than $22, however, the federal government would not pay for the excess—then there was no federal ceiling on the amount the state might have to pay for welfare during the year. In other words, the linkage of the federal portion of supplementary payments to state standards in January 1972 placed limits on federal SSI payments. If the federal government had not established such a link, but instead had restricted a state's fiscal liability to an amount of money that was independent of payment standards, the states could have been induced to expand their supplementary standards.

The provision offering the states financial protection against escalating supplementary payments is known as the "hold-harmless" clause. This clause was originally scheduled to phase out as the federal SSI standard increased because of cost-of-living adjustments and approached the January 1972 standard.[6] When the SSI standard reached the 1972 state standard, the federal government would absorb the full cost of current payments based on 1972 standards. Thus, if a state had not raised its payment standards above 1972 levels, none of its own resources would have been used to make payments to the aged, blind, and disabled.

The Department of Health, Education, and Welfare's application of the hold-harmless provision has been said to be contrary to legislative intent.[7] Although the 1972 amendments require the states to

---

[6] The hold-harmless clause is discussed more fully in *Federal Register*, vol. 40 (February 21, 1975), pp. 7639–47. States would be held harmless at their 1972 levels of expenditures if the above conditions were satisfied.

[7] U.S. Congress, Senate, Committee on Finance, *The Supplemental Security Income Program*, 95th Congress, 1st session, April 1977, pp. 71–75.

pay for supplementary payments that raise an individual recipient's welfare income above the amount paid to a person in 1972 (APL), the program is not operating in this manner. Instead, in calculating federal participation in supplementary costs, payments above the APL are netted against payments below the APL. As a result, in several states, "the Federal Government is picking up the tab for State Supplementary payments far in excess of the adjusted payment level."[8] This policy may have raised federal expenditures above levels intended by the Congress and affected both the level and the composition of supplementary payments.

In addition to hold-harmless protection, the states were offered the option of federal administration of supplementary payments, with the federal government absorbing the cost of federally administered supplements.[9] The states and the District of Columbia spent $162 million in 1973 to administer welfare programs for the aged, blind, and disabled. Annual administrative costs in seven states were at least $5 million, mounting to $37 million in California and $30 million in New York.[10] Federal administration of the supplements would have saved the states the portion of the 1973 costs otherwise spent to administer supplementary payments.

Level of State Saving. The change in the financing of welfare payments for the aged, blind, and disabled presented the states with a choice between fiscal relief or expanded welfare programs. States wishing to maximize fiscal relief would replace their own welfare payments with federal payments. At the extreme, states in which SSI payment levels were above former levels could completely end their welfare payments to these groups. States electing to provide additional welfare as a result of the new federal program would forgo fiscal relief.

The federal government estimated that the SSI program would save the states in excess of $853 million.[11] This estimate includes the

---

[8] Ibid., p. 72.

[9] A state's decision to elect federal or state administration is not irreversible. Administrative responsibility for supplementation can be changed 120 days after the secretary of Health, Education, and Welfare is notified of the state's intention. During the first two years of the program, several states switched from federal administration to state administration or vice versa. See Sue Hawkins, "State Supplementation under SSI, 1974," *Social Security Bulletin*, vol. 40 (February 1977), pp. 12–20; and Social Security Administration, "State Supplementation under the SSI Program, Calendar Year 1974," *Research and Statistics Note*, note 6 (April 16, 1976).

[10] Unpublished data provided by the Social Security Administration.

[11] U.S. Congress, Senate, Committee on Finance, *Social Security Amendments of 1972*, 92nd Congress, 2nd session, September 26, 1972, pp. 532–34.

cost of mandatory but not optional state supplementary payments. Moreover, the cost of making supplementary payments to persons whose incomes were below 1973 welfare standards, but who did not receive assistance in that year, was placed at approximately $100 million. Net savings were therefore estimated to be approximately $750 million. Virtually every state was expected to share in the savings. California was to save $177 million; New York, $79 million; and Massachusetts, $20 million.[12]

Despite SSI, twelve states (Alaska, California, Colorado, Massachusetts, Michigan, Nevada, New York, Oklahoma, Pennsylvania, Rhode Island, Vermont, and Wisconsin) actually spent more for welfare for the aged, blind, and disabled in 1976 than 1973. Some increases were large: in California, a $414 million increase (104 percent); in Massachusetts, $42 million (66 percent); and in New York, $42 million (22 percent).[13] In addition, total federal welfare payments for these states in 1976 amounted to $1.7 billion, up 93 percent from $0.9 billion in 1973.[14] Thirty-eight states spent less for welfare, however, saving from $100,000 to $35.9 million. The total savings in these states amounted to $345.1 million.

Table 23 shows the change in the amount states spent for welfare payments to the aged, blind, and disabled between 1973 and 1976. As shown in column 2, twelve states reduced their payments by at least 93 percent, many others by more than 60 percent. In 1976, therefore, many states used little of their own resources for welfare payments to the aged, blind, and disabled. In Texas, the state constitution prohibits supplementary payments. In general, as columns 3 and 4 of Table 23 show, the proportionate decline in state spending was largest in the states that had relatively low payment standards in 1973 and did not supplement federal payment standards. Welfare recipients in these states, however, realized substantial increases in their welfare income because of SSI, even though there was a sharp reduction in welfare payments financed by the states.

SSI provided comparatively little fiscal relief for states with high

---

[12] Estimated by apportioning the $100 million to the states in proportion to their share of the $853 million.

[13] Unpublished data provided by the Social Security Administration.

[14] In the same way, a federal takeover of Assistance to Families with Dependent Children (AFDC) and other welfare programs may not provide every state with relief. For a study claiming that federalization of the AFDC programs would lower assistance payments, see Larry L. Orr, "Income Transfers as a Public Good: An Application to AFDC," *American Economic Review*, vol. 66 (June 1976), pp. 359–71. Also see Committee for Economic Development, *Welfare Reform and Its Financing* (New York, 1976).

TABLE 23

Change in State Share of Public Assistance and SSI Payments between Calendar Years 1973 and 1976

Region/State	Change in State Payments		Change in State Share of Payments	
	Amount (millions of dollars)	Percent	Percentage points	Percent
	(1)	(2)	(3)	(4)
United States	180.1	13.3	−15	− 37.5
Region I				
Connecticut	− 3.0	− 25.0	−26	− 52.0
Maine	− 1.0	− 15.9	− 9	− 30.0
Massachusetts	42.2	65.7	− 2	− 4.0
New Hampshire	− 1.1	− 34.4	−12	− 30.0
Rhode Island	0.9	18.4	−18	− 38.3
Vermont	1.4	51.9	− 2	− 5.7
Total	39.4	42.2	− 6	− 12.8
Region II				
New Jersey	− 0.8	− 3.5	−31	− 62.0
New York	41.9	21.5	−15	− 30.0
Total	41.1	18.9	−18	− 36.0
Region III				
Delaware	− 2.2	− 73.3	−40	− 80.0
District of Columbia	− 9.6	− 96.0	−48	− 96.0
Maryland	−12.3	− 93.2	−40	− 97.6
Pennsylvania	20.4	53.7	−21	− 46.7
Virginia	− 9.7	− 89.0	−36	− 97.3
West Virginia	− 6.7	−100.0	−25	−100.0
Total	−20.1	− 24.6	−28	− 68.3
Region IV				
Alabama	−16.0	− 60.8	−17	− 73.9
Florida[a]	−19.5	− 92.4	−27	− 96.4
Georgia	−21.3	− 93.8	−23	− 95.8
Kentucky	− 7.8	− 43.3	−19	− 70.4
Mississippi	−13.5	− 96.4	−17	− 94.4
North Carolina	− 2.2	− 11.2	−20	− 69.0
South Carolina	− 4.5	− 81.8	−23	− 95.8
Tennessee	−13.8	− 98.6	−23	− 95.8
Total	−98.6	− 69.8	−21	− 87.5
Region V				
Illinois	−33.8	− 50.4	−34	− 68.0
Indiana	− 4.7	− 90.4	−28	− 96.6
Michigan	6.0	11.5	−19	− 38.0
Minnesota	− 7.0	− 59.8	−32	− 74.4

TABLE 23—Continued

Region/State	Change in State Payments		Change in State Share of Payments	
	Amount (millions of dollars)	Percent	Percentage points	Percent
	(1)	(2)	(3)	(4)
Ohio	−35.9	− 90.9	−44	− 95.7
Wisconsin	3.6	22.5	−20	− 47.6
Total	−71.8	− 37.4	−31	− 66.0
Region VI				
Arkansas	−12.8	− 94.1	−21	− 95.5
Louisiana	−25.3	− 90.3	−24	− 96.0
New Mexico	− 3.9	−100.0	−26	−100.0
Oklahoma	2.2	9.9	−10	− 32.3
Texas	−35.9	−100.0	−25	−100.0
Total	−75.7	− 73.1	−22	− 84.6
Region VII				
Iowa	− 4.6	− 78.0	−37	− 90.2
Kansas	− 5.2	− 94.5	−42	− 97.7
Missouri	−12.3	− 38.0	−16	− 51.6
Nebraska	− 2.4	− 45.3	−26	− 63.4
Total	−24.5	− 49.9	−22	− 64.7
Region VIII				
Arizona	− 7.2	− 84.7	−13	− 30.2
Colorado	0.7	4.3	−33	− 91.7
Montana	− 1.3	− 72.2	−27	− 81.8
North Dakota	− 1.9	− 95.0	−28	− 96.6
South Dakota	− 0.9	− 69.2	−25	− 86.2
Utah	− 2.2	−100.0	−29	− 96.7
Wyoming	− 0.7	−100.0	−37	−100.0
Total	−13.5	− 41.4	−23	− 62.2
Region IX				
California	414.2	104.4	10	20.0
Hawaii	− 0.5	− 12.5	−25	− 51.0
Nevada	1.5	166.0	− 5	− 14.3
Total	415.2	103.4	9	18.0
Region X				
Alaska	0.2	6.5	− 7	− 14.0
Idaho	− 0.1	− 5.0	−13	− 43.3
Oregon	− 3.0	− 38.0	−28	− 66.7
Washington	− 8.5	− 35.3	−28	− 58.3
Total	−11.4	− 30.7	−25	− 55.6

[a] Based on 1973 payments of $47 million for the aged in contrast with $67 million shown in Appendix, Table A-5. Other figures also differed slightly.

SOURCE: Unpublished data furnished by the Social Security Administration.

TABLE 24

Comparison of SSI Payments in 1976 with Public Assistance Payments in 1973 for States with a High Percentage of People Receiving State Supplementation Only

(percent)

State	Percent of People with State Supplementation Only	1976 Total Payments as a Percent of 1973 Payments	1976 State Share of Payments as a Percent of 1973 State Share of Payments
Massachusetts	41.4	185.9	98.4
California	35.8	201.0	119.0
Wisconsin	32.1	93.4	51.9
Maine	22.8	105.4	75.2
Nevada	21.0	300.0	100.3
Rhode Island	18.5	118.4	60.0
Colorado	17.5	99.4	69.3
Vermont	17.2	63.0	99.2
New York	17.1	138.9	71.2
Alaska	16.4	96.9	78.7
Connecticut	15.8	63.2	47.6
Average for rest of the United States	2.4	46.7	25.5

Source: Alicia H. Munnell and Ann M. Connolly, "Federalizing Welfare: The Fiscal Impact of the SSI Program," *New England Economic Review*, September-October 1977, p. 15.

payment standards in 1973, partly because many SSI recipients received only state supplementary payments in 1976 since their countable income was too high for federal payments. Indeed, for many recipients, the state cost of supplementation was greater than the state share of payments under the old program. Table 24 shows the states with over 15 percent of their SSI recipients with state supplements only and compares these percentages with the ratio of 1976 payments to 1973 payments. Clearly, a high proportion of "supplementation only" recipients "is coincident with little reduction in either state dollar costs or the state's share of total costs."[15] Most noticeable

[15] Alicia H. Munnell and Ann M. Connolly, "Federalizing Welfare: The Fiscal Impact of the SSI Program," *New England Economic Review* (September-October, 1977), p. 14.

is the relationship in Massachusetts and California, where more than one-third of the recipients received state supplementary payments only.

SSI also did not provide some states with fiscal relief because they chose to increase their payment standards above 1972 levels. Until 1976, states with standards above the federal standard could not pass along federal cost-of-living adjustments without simultaneously incurring a reduction in the amount of supplementary payments paid for by the federal government. The federal government treated the pass-along as a state-initiated increase that raised the payment standard above the January 1972 level. Hence if these states wished to maintain the purchasing power of the federal standard, they had to do so at their own expense. These states were also financially liable if they adjusted their supplementary standards to fluctuations in prices. It was inevitable that over time these states would raise their standards and thus incur higher welfare payments.

In October 1976 federal legislation froze the remaining amount of hold-harmless protection at its 1976 level. This freeze means that federal cost-of-living adjustments could henceforth be passed along at federal expense—that is, they will no longer be treated as state-initiated increases in payment standards above the 1972 levels.[16] Nothing was done about the diminution in the state's financial protection that occurred between 1974 and 1976. During this time, the aggregate protection declined from $211 million in fiscal year 1975 to $63 million in calendar year 1976. California lost $70 million in protection; New York, $63 million; and Massachusetts, $14 million.[17] Inflation adjustments to the supplementary standards, however, will continue to be at state expense.

The savings a state realized may not have translated into tax relief for its residents. Since the SSI program increased federal welfare payments, the decrease in a particular state's outlays for welfare programs may have been offset by a concurrent rise in federal taxes. It has been estimated that in fiscal year 1976 about half the $15 million decrease in Mississippi's taxing requirements for welfare for the aged, blind, and disabled were canceled by additional federal taxes. In contrast, not only did state taxes for welfare for these groups rise in California by $374 million, but Californians had to pay another $200 million to finance the new program at the federal level.[18]

---

[16] More precisely, each state is required to maintain total supplements at the December 1976 level. States are not legally required to pass along the entire cost-of-living adjustment if supplementary payments in the present year would exceed the payments in the previous year.

[17] Unpublished data provided by the Social Security Administration.

[18] Munnell and Connolly, "Federalizing Welfare," pp. 13–14.

Effect of SSI on the Distribution of Federal Revenues

SSI also affected the distribution of federal revenues between high-income and low-income states. In 1973 the federal government's share of welfare payments for the aged, blind, and disabled ranged from 50 percent in high-income states to 82 percent in low-income states—percentages that were usually designated before funds were spent. Under the SSI program, the federal share was not specifically linked to state per capita income and was not stipulated beforehand. Instead, the federal percentage depended primarily on interrelationships among the number of recipients, payment standards, and state supplementary payments.

Federal outlays for welfare payments to the aged, blind, and disabled increased from $2 billion in 1973 to $4.6 billion in 1976. Federal per capita payments per person eighteen years and over rose from $14.05 in 1973 to $31.06 in 1976, while the federal share of the payments rose from 60 percent to 75 percent, increasing in every state in the nation except California (where it was down 10 percentage points). Table 25 indicates that these changes were accompanied by a relative shift in the distribution of federal welfare dollars among regions. The most striking change is the shift from the West to the South. On a statewide basis, there was a relative shift of money from California to Florida, South Carolina, Virginia, and other southern states. Hence, not only did southern states spend little of their own resources for welfare programs for the aged, blind, and disabled in 1976, but they also received a larger share of the increase in federal spending. These changes adhere to the objective of SSI to relieve the

TABLE 25

PERCENTAGE DISTRIBUTION OF THE FEDERAL SHARE OF WELFARE
PAYMENTS BY CENSUS REGION, 1973 AND 1976

Census Region[a]	1973	1976
Northeast	18.6	19.7
North Central	16.1	17.5
South	39.9	45.4
West	25.4	17.4
All regions	100.0	100.0

[a] Classifications by the U.S. Bureau of the Census.
SOURCE: Unpublished data provided by the Social Security Administration.

states of the financial burden of welfare costs while concurrently making the payments among states more equitable.

Effect of SSI on the Cost of Medicaid

Part of the fiscal relief offered to the states by SSI may have been counterbalanced by SSI-induced increases in the portion of Medicaid payments paid for by the states. In 1973 most welfare recipients were automatically eligible for Medicaid benefits. This changed on January 1, 1974, because the states were not required to cover all SSI recipients for Medicaid. Instead, a state was required to offer Medicaid services only to SSI recipients meeting January 1972 eligibility criteria. Table A-1 in the Appendix shows that in July 1978 fourteen states used 1972 standards to determine Medicaid eligibility.[19]

The 1972 amendments gave a state the option of having the Social Security Administration determine Medicaid eligibility—in order to avoid duplicative determinations of eligibility—if the state accepted SSI eligibility as a condition for Medicaid benefits. In July 1978 the Social Security Administration determined Medicaid eligibility for twenty-eight states. These states, however, are required to determine whether individuals who are ineligible for SSI, such as residents of public domiciliary facilities, may be eligible for Medicaid.

The addition of newly entitled aged, blind, and disabled persons to the Medicaid roles increased Medicaid payments. In certain instances the cost increases may have been large because there was no hold-harmless protection against increases in Medicaid payments. In addition, some states had to hire new staff or establish new units to handle the increased caseload. Data processing costs increased, especially in states that were dissatisfied with the format, accuracy, and timeliness of the information transmitted by the Social Security Administration. In many cases persons requiring medical attention found it difficult to obtain services because they failed to receive timely certification of their Medicaid eligibility. On the other hand,

---

[19] SSI recipients who failed to meet 1972 resource standards could still obtain Medicaid services, however, after spending their excess income for health care and divesting themselves of excess resources. Further, Medicaid coverage could be extended to non-SSI aged, blind, and disabled persons after they spent their excess income on health care.

The timing and manner in which resources are divested raises important policy questions. The Social Security Administration permits adults to transfer resources to their children and subsequently become eligible for Medicaid. See U.S. Congress, House of Representatives, Subcommittee on Oversight and Investigation of the Committee on Interstate and Foreign Commerce, *Problems of Medicaid Fraud and Abuse*, 94th Congress, 2nd session, February 13, 1976, p. 115.

TABLE 26

ESTIMATED EFFECTS OF SSI ON STATE MEDICAID PROGRAMS IN REGION IV

State	Number of Aged, Blind, and Disabled Medicaid Recipients		Estimated Increase in State Share of Medicaid Payments because of SSI Program		All SSI Recipients Eligible for Medicaid
	1973 (thousands)	1975 (thousands)	Amount (millions of dollars)	Percent of calendar year 1973 payments	
Alabama	133.7	162.2	7.8	11.3	yes
Florida	95.0	140.8	15.7	22.3	yes
Georgia	158.6	173.6	10.6	10.0	yes
Kentucky	111.2	119.8	4.7	9.5	yes
Mississippi	109.7	117.3	1.3	2.9	no
North Carolina	133.3	170.4	0.0	0.0	no
South Carolina	50.1	118.4	4.7	16.1	yes
Tennessee	83.6	134.5	9.3	18.2	yes

SOURCES: Numbers of recipients from U.S. Department of Health, Education, and Welfare, *Numbers of Recipients and Amounts of Payments under Medicaid, Fiscal Year 1973*, table 2, and *State Tables, Fiscal Year 1975, Medicaid: Recipients, Payments and Services* (1978), table 2; Medicaid eligibility from Social Security Administration, *Supplemental Security Income for the Aged, Blind, and Disabled: Summary of State Payment Levels, State Supplementation, and Medicaid Decisions* (July 1975). Payments from various issues of U.S. Department of Health, Education, and Welfare, *Medical Assistance (Medicaid) Financed under Title XIX of the Social Security Act*, table 3.

many persons obtained services they were not entitled to receive because of the high error rate associated with SSI eligibility determinations (see Chapter 5).

SSI was more likely to increase Medicaid payments in states that in 1973 had provided Medicaid benefits only to persons who were receiving federally matched welfare payments but then elected to cover all SSI recipients. Conversely, the effects were more likely to be unimportant in states that previously had a Medicaid program that extended benefits to low-income persons who were not welfare recipients and subsequently restricted eligibility to SSI recipients meeting January 1972 standards. Tentative estimates of the impact of SSI on Medicaid payments in eight southern states are shown in Table 26.[20] With two exceptions, these states seem to have used a large portion of their fiscal relief from welfare payments to expand their Medicaid umbrella. Florida and South Carolina received almost no net relief because of SSI-induced increases in Medicaid payments.[21]

---

[20] To estimate the effect of the new program on Medicaid payments, it was necessary to predict 1975 payments without SSI. This task was complicated by several factors. First, since the health industry was under price controls from August 1971 to April 1974, Medicaid reimbursement rates during this interval could not be used to forecast 1975 rates. Second, between 1974 and 1975 many states restricted the utilization of certain services, while some states expanded their benefit package. Third, since the 1972 amendments extended Medicare coverage to qualified disabled persons, Medicare began reimbursing several health services previously financed by Medicaid. Fourth, the new law required the states to implement changes which affected utilization and reimbursement rates. Fifth, the utilization patterns of newly eligible recipients may have differed from those of the grandfathered recipients.

Because of these difficulties and data limitations, somewhat arbitrary procedures were employed to estimate Medicaid payments without SSI. Estimates for the ith group in the jth state were calculated by raising actual 1974 payments for the first half of the calendar year by estimated changes in health prices (ΔP), recipients (ΔR), and utilization (ΔU) for the next 18 months. ΔP was set at the change in the medical care component of the CPI; this change was especially large during the nine months following the lifting of price controls in April 1974. ΔU was arbitrarily estimated at 3 percent. ΔR was estimated at 2 percent for the aged and 7 percent for the disabled based on an examination of the number of recipients in fiscal years 1970 through 1975. For additional discussion, see Paul L. Grimaldi, "Fiscal and Distributive Impacts of the Supplemental Security Income Program," *Review of Social Economy*, vol. 36 (October 1978), pp. 192–93. Also, see Sue C. Hawkins and Donald E. Rigby, "Effect of SSI on Medicaid Caseloads and Expenditures," *Social Security Bulletin*, vol. 42 (February 1979), pp. 3–14.

[21] If some of the people who became eligible for Medicaid because of SSI had been receiving health care under other programs, part of the increase in Medicaid payments might not represent new state expenditures.

5

Administrative Efficiency of SSI

The state-administered welfare programs for the aged, blind, and disabled that existed before SSI are widely recognized to have been enmeshed in a bewildering patchwork of rules, regulations, policies, and procedures. Costly delays, mistakes, intergovernmental strife, recipient frustration, and taxpayer complaints were common occurrences. A major argument in favor of SSI was that the federal government would do a better administrative job than the states. The Social Security Administration was made responsible for administering the new program because many SSI recipients would also be drawing social security benefits. In addition, the Congress hoped that the widespread favorable public image of the social security system would reduce the stigma often associated with being on welfare and would also encourage eligible persons to enroll in the program.[1]

Having the Social Security Administration administer the program was hailed as the solution to the "welfare mess" and the "ineptitudes of incompetent state administrators." Former Secretary of Health, Education, and Welfare Elliott B. Richardson testified in 1971:

---

[1] One poll of 1,447 persons found that the public disapproves of welfare under that name. Fifty-eight percent of the respondents disapproved of most government-sponsored welfare programs, and more than half believed that most recipients could get along without welfare if they really tried. After the word "welfare" was deleted from certain questions, however, most respondents agreed with the purposes of welfare programs. Over four-fifths supported food stamps and health care for the poor and cash assistance for young families. See *New York Times*, August 3, 1977, pp. A-1 and D-15. Perhaps this sensitivity partly explains why SSI payments are often referred to as "benefits" and recipients as "beneficiaries," which imply that welfare income has been earned or is a matter of right rather than a handout.

But when it comes to a function such as the determination of eligibility under a uniform national program, the computation of benefits, the cross-checking of income data to determine whether or not it has been accurately set forth in the application form, or the processing of checks, we think the Federal Government has established a very good track record of capacity and, indeed, that this is a kind of function that can be performed with considerably greater efficiency on a uniform national basis, than it can be done by the States or localities.[2]

Social Security Administration personnel predicted that the new program, with its anticipated doubling in caseload, would require only half the number of persons previously employed by state and local governments:

States now report 32,000 state and local income maintenance employees handling 3.3 million aged, blind, and disabled cases. By January 1974, there will be an estimated 6.3 million cases in these categories. SSA has received approved [sic] for an additional 15,000 new positions by January 1, 1974, to handle this workload.[3]

The Social Security Administration estimated that federal administration would save $110 million. Most of these savings were not realized, however, because the Social Security Administration underestimated its staffing needs. In contrast with the estimated increase of 15,000 employees, the Social Security Administration had 22,000 SSI employees in 1976, even though the SSI caseload was half the expected number.[4]

Insufficient Lead Time

Many people believe that there was too little lead time to plan for and implement the SSI program. According to Social Security Administration Commissioner James B. Cardwell, "When the program became operational in January 1974, all of the systems needed to execute and update claims and payments were not available."[5] As a result,

---

[2] U.S. Congress, Senate, Committee on Finance, *The Supplemental Security Income Program*, 95th Congress, 1st session, April 1977, p. 45.

[3] U.S. Congress, House of Representatives, Subcommittee on Oversight of the Committee on Ways and Means, *Administration of the Supplemental Security Income Program*, vol. 5, 94th Congress, 2nd session, October 20, 1976, p. 22.

[4] Ibid.

[5] Ibid., vol. 2, p. 2.

there were delays in determining eligibility and a substantial waste of taxpayer dollars.[6]

> It was apparent even before the first payment was made, and later confirmed, that the accounting system had many shortcomings and lacked adherence to several generally accepted accounting principles. Totals were not balanced from one part of the processing to another. Amounts certified to the Treasury Department for payment to recipients were not supported at the earliest possible point to provide a predetermined total to verify that the correct amount was certified for payment. Accurate accounting distributions were not provided for billing State agencies and charging the Federal appropriation. Accounting data were not generated for all types of actions taken. An over and under-payment system was non-operative.[7]

The Social Security Administration could have deferred implementation or elected to implement SSI gradually, but instead it assumed control on January 1, 1974. Several reasons have been advanced to explain the ensuing problems. First, the changeover from state administration to federal administration was complicated by changes in personnel in the Department of Health, Education, and Welfare between October 1972 and January 1, 1974. During that time, a secretary and undersecretary, and other key policy makers assumed office. The new appointees had different ideas and philosophies, and it took time for them to become acquainted with SSI and other related programs. Second, conflicts between federal and state agencies and within federal agencies slowed the administrative transition. Numerous state officials resented federal intrusion into their programs and were upset by what they perceived as federal employees chiding them for alleged administrative inefficiencies. Third, the Social Security Administration underestimated the administrative problems inherent in making pay-

---

[6] A 1977 survey of the public's views and suggestions concerning welfare reform of the Assistance to Families with Dependent Children (AFDC) and other programs found that "generally, the early problems in administering the SSI program influenced opinions [about federal administration]. For instance, some of the nationally known and most respected people in the social work/public assistance community, who had consistently espoused the cause of federal administration in the past, in some instances for decades, indicated current misgivings about this approach." See U.S. Department of Health, Education, and Welfare, *Welfare Reform: Final National Summary Report on Regional Outreach* (April 15, 1977), p. E-3.

[7] U.S. Congress, House of Representatives, Subcommittee on Oversight of the Committee on Ways and Means, *Oversight of the Supplemental Security Income Program*, 94th Congress, 2nd session, April 8 and May 6, 1976, pp. 176–77.

TABLE 27

PERCENTAGE OF SSI CASES WITH ERRORS, 1974–1976

Type of Error	July–December 1974	January–June 1975	July–December 1975	January–June 1976
Overpayments	13.3	11.0	9.9	9.4
Payments to ineligibles	6.1	7.7	8.1	7.8
Underpayments	5.4	5.7	6.1	5.6
Total error rate	24.8	24.4	24.1	22.8

SOURCE: U.S. Congress, Senate, Committee on Finance, *The Supplemental Security Income Program*, 95th Congress, 1st session, April 1977, p. 49.

ments under "means-tested" programs. This was partly the result of misconceptions stemming from the comparatively routinized eligibility and payment procedures under the Old Age, Survivors, and Disability Insurance program (OASDI). Fourth, the Congress intensified administrative complexities by modifying the enabling legislation a few times before SSI was launched. Fifth, the Social Security Administration may not have had sufficient resources to develop supportive administrative systems.

Error Rate

The Social Security Administration has a quality assurance program to test the administrative efficiency of SSI. This program employs sampling techniques to gauge administrative performance and to determine how efficiently the program is operating. Each month a random sample of 5,000 cases is selected to determine the causes, extent, and cost of payment errors. SSI recipients are interviewed at home to determine if they are receiving the proper SSI payment.

Table 27 shows that quality assurance has consistently reported an error rate of almost 25 percent; that is, one out of every four claims contains a payment error. This rate approximates the pre-SSI rate for the state-administered programs and varies considerably among federal regions, ranging from 19.3 percent in Region VII to 34.4 percent in Region I for the last half of calendar year 1975.[8] A portion of the early SSI error rates is attributable to inaccuracies in the records that the states transferred to the Social Security Admin-

---

[8] Ibid., pp. 49–50.

istration; 24.6 percent of all transferred cases for which the Social Security Administration did not redetermine eligibility contained inaccuracies. Nevertheless, an analysis of errors by type of case shows that through September 30, 1975, over 30 percent of the claims handled exclusively by the Social Security Administration had errors.[9] Even after the Social Security Administration redetermined eligibility for a transferred case, the error rate was 15.7 percent.[10]

The incidence of errors is actually larger than reported above. The quality assurance program does not include errors caused by mistakes in determining the severity of an impairment or condition for SSI disability payments. Social Security Administration records indicate that 20 percent of all SSI disability determinations are based upon incomplete information. In addition, the Social Security Administration does not count as an error an overpayment or underpayment of less than $5 a month. If the Social Security Administration overpaid all SSI recipients by $4.99 a month for an entire year, its reported error rate would be zero, even though it would have misspent $240 million! It would seem, therefore, that the tolerance limit ought to be reduced in order to provide a better measure of the accuracy of the program in dispensing payments. As soon as accurate information is available and is cross-tabulated by cause of error and category of recipient, the Social Security Administration will be better able to allocate resources efficiently for corrective actions.

High error rates do not necessarily mean that Social Security Administration personnel are responsible for incorrect payments. A major problem is in processing reported changes in assets, income, and other factors affecting eligibility or payments. Another is that recipients sometimes fail to provide the Social Security Administration with timely notification of a change in financial circumstances or living arrangements. Also, potentially eligible individuals may supply the Social Security Administration with inaccurate information, or situations may arise in which an overpayment cannot be adjusted until the recipient has an opportunity for a fair hearing. It is estimated that about 50 percent of the errors involve misstatements about non-assistance income, while an additional 20 percent concern living arrangements. No figures are available to show what proportion of errors were generated by the Social Security Administration and what proportion were generated by recipients.

---

[9] Ibid., pp. 166–68.

[10] In January 1976, Commissioner Cardwell testified that he did not believe the error rate would fall below 15 percent without costly legislative changes. See Senate, Committee on Finance, *The Supplemental Security Income Program*, p. 83, n. 1.

Social Security Administration records indicate that SSI recipients were overpaid $913 million during the first three years of the program. Estimates based on the quality assurance program for July 1974 to June 1976 indicate overpayments of $1.2 billion, or 30 percent more than the administration's records indicate for three years. Most of these overpayments will probably not be recovered because the Social Security Administration has waived or deferred collection efforts because of staffing shortages. Furthermore, the financial consequence of the errors remains large more than four years after the advent of SSI. The Social Security Administration estimates that between January 1976 and March 1978 it overpaid $1 billion and underpaid $262 million for an average monthly net overpayment of $27 million or about 5 percent of payments.[11]

States have reacted to the high error rates by withholding partial reimbursement for federally administered supplementary payments. Several states with state-administered supplements have also expressed discontent with federal inaccuracies. More than half the states withheld a total of $70 million for fiscal year 1975; New York withheld $36 million and California $16 million.[12] The Social Security Administration has made efforts to resolve the disputed amounts and, in certain circumstances, has considered terminating its contract with a state because the state failed to compensate the federal government for all federally administered supplementary payments. The 1977 amendments to the Social Security Act partially resolve the disputes by directing the Department of Health, Education, and Welfare to reimburse the states for state-administered supplementary payments that an HEW audit finds were incorrectly made in 1974 because the state relied in good faith on information furnished by HEW.

Fraud and Abuse

Some errors may be attributable to fraud and abuse on the part of recipients, the Social Security Administration, or state employees.[13]

---

[11] General Accounting Office, *Erroneous Supplemental Security Income Payments Result from Problems in Processing Changes in Recipients' Circumstances*, Report to Joseph A. Califano, Jr., Secretary, Department of Health, Education, and Welfare (February 16, 1979). Monthly error data in Social Security Administration, *SSI Statistics*, table 13.

[12] U.S. Congress, House of Representatives, Subcommittee on Public Assistance of the Committee on Ways and Means, *Supplemental Security Income Program*, vol. 1, 94th Congress, 1st session, June 3, 1975, pp. 28–29.

[13] As of early 1976, no fraud had been detected among Social Security Administration employees, while two cases were reported for welfare workers in two states.

Between July 1973 and July 1975 about 5,900 potential recipient fraud cases were referred to regional offices for investigation. Each of these cases may be referred for prosecution, pending the results of an investigation. Prosecution may not follow, however, because of either a backlog of more serious crimes or sympathy for the aged and physically impaired. As of December 1975, nineteen persons had been convicted of recipient fraud. Some were convicted of misdemeanors punishable by fines up to $1,000 and/or imprisonment for not more than one year. A few were convicted of felonies.

6

The Relationship of SSI to OASDHI

The Old Age, Survivors, Disability, and Health Insurance program (OASDHI) plays an enormous role in providing income security for the elderly and disabled. About 34 million people currently receive old age, survivors, or disability benefits. This chapter focuses on how the SSI program presents policy makers with an opportunity to develop a social security program in which benefits are more closely related to earnings.[1]

The OASDHI Program

Entitlement to social security benefits is earned through the payment of employee and employer payroll taxes; benefits are paid to retirees, survivors, or the disabled irrespective of need. Although benefits vary directly with a worker's earnings, the relationship between earnings and benefits is imperfect. The benefit structure is progressive—heavily weighted in favor of low-income workers on the assumption that persons with high incomes during their working years are better able to save for their retirement years than are low-income workers. There are also provisions for a minimum benefit, a larger benefit for a re-

---

[1] Shortly before the SSI program was launched, the former chief actuary of the Social Security Administration pondered whether SSI would have major adverse effects on social security: "The big questions about SSI will not be answered for years to come. Will it result only in a more equitable and adequate treatment of the low-income aged, blind, and disabled? Or will it be a sleeping giant which, when aroused, will destroy or diminish both Social Security and private economic-security measures?" See Robert J. Myers, "With SSI, Who Needs Social Security?" *Challenge*, vol. 16 (November-December 1973), p. 61. Also, see Martha N. Ozawa, "SSI: Progress or Retreat?" *Public Welfare* (Spring 1974), pp. 33–40; and James R. Storey, "The New Supplemental Security Income—Implications for Other Benefit Programs," *Policy Sciences*, vol. 6 (1975), pp. 359–74.

tired worker with an aged wife than for a single person, and more favorable treatment for self-employed persons than for employees.

The benefit structure mirrors two objectives of the social security program: social adequacy and individual equity. Social adequacy relates to whether social security benefits provide a socially acceptable level of income for beneficiaries. Individual equity is concerned with the actuarial relationship between payroll taxes and social security benefits. The closer the benefits and taxes, the more equitable the system since workers receive benefits according to the payroll taxes they and their employers paid.

Social adequacy and individual equity are, however, conflicting goals. Whenever the Congress has improved the adequacy of benefits by raising the minimum benefit or making the benefit structure progressive, for example, the relationship between taxes and benefits has weakened. The original Social Security Act was described as an insurance system, and the principal emphasis was on individual equity. Before the first checks were mailed, however, the Congress amended the act to include a progressive benefit formula because of concern about the small size of the benefits that an earnings-related system would pay to persons reaching age sixty-five in the early years of the program. The progressive benefit formula violates the principle of individual equity and introduces a welfare component into the social security program. This component can be defined as the "part of the benefits paid that have little or no relationship to the covered worker's earnings and the payroll-tax contributions paid on these earnings."[2] The resulting inequities did not raise serious problems so long as social security benefits were small.[3] As the benefits have increased, the financial significance of the inequities has become more apparent and has led many people to wonder whether social security is a "bad buy"—whether the benefits are overpriced relative to similar protection that is or could be made available by private companies.[4]

The social security program has made an immense contribution

---

[2] George E. Rejda, *Social Insurance and Economic Security* (Englewood Cliffs, N.J.: Prentice-Hall, 1976), p. 35.

[3] Unearned benefits represent at least one-third of OASDHI benefits. See U.S. Congress, House of Representatives, Committee on Ways and Means, *Reports of the 1971 Advisory Council on Social Security*, 92nd Congress, 1st session, 1971, p. 5.

[4] Some people suggest that one indication of the "bad buy" is the number of state and local governments opting to withdraw from the system. As of 1976, about 45,000 nonfederal public employees had left the system and applications were pending for an additional 53,000 workers. Most of these workers are employed by small local governments. See Robert J. Myers, "Should State and Local Governments Desert the Social Security Ship?" *Tax Foundation's Tax Review,*

toward eliminating poverty among elderly persons if poverty is measured by a threshold rather than relative to the incomes of other age groups.[5] The Congressional Budget Office estimates that 38 percent of all aged families in 1976, or 64 percent of the aged poor, were removed from poverty largely by social security benefits. A substantial portion of social security income, however, went to persons who were not poor. In 1976, for example, social security helped to double the proportion—from 31.7 percent to 61.7 percent—of aged families whose gross income was at least 50 percent above the poverty level.[6] Similar findings are supported by unpublished census data shown in Table 28. In 1976, over 60 percent of families with an aged head receiving social security had incomes of at least $7,000 and 21 percent had incomes of more than $15,000. The majority of aged unrelated individuals also had incomes above the poverty threshold. It seems clear, therefore, that an across-the-board increase in social security is no longer an effective and efficient way to help the neediest aged persons. Rather, future efforts to abolish poverty among the elderly would be more efficient if they were channeled through a means-tested program such as SSI.[7]

Not all of an across-the-board increase in SSI payments would go to poor elderly persons.[8] Some of the increase, although less than

---

vol. 33 (November 1976), pp. 37–40. For an alternative proposal, see James M. Buchanan, "Social Insurance in a Growing Economy: A Proposal for Radical Reform," *National Tax Journal*, vol. 21 (December 1968), pp. 386–95.

[5] The original purpose of the social security program was to provide retirement income to supplement private pensions, other income, and savings. Today, many people contend that its purpose is to prevent poverty among retirees. Note the viewpoint of the three labor representatives on the Quadrennial Advisory Council: "In keeping its attention riveted on cost factors and the hypothetical tripartite system of income protection, the Council has given inadequate attention to the social adequacy of benefit levels and the need to raise benefits. Until benefits are raised, the true purpose of Social Security—*to prevent poverty among the aged*—will not be realized" (emphasis added). U.S. Congress, House of Representatives, Communication from Secretary of Health, Education, and Welfare, *Reports of the Quadrennial Advisory Council on Social Security*, 94th Congress, 1st session, March 10, 1975, p. 69.

[6] Congressional Budget Office, *Poverty Status of Families under Alternative Definitions of Income* (June 1977), tables 6 and A-8.

[7] Plotnick and Skidmore estimate that 58 percent of the across-the-board social security increases between 1970 and 1972 did not close poverty gaps; see Robert D. Plotnick and Felicity Skidmore, *Progress against Poverty: A Review of the 1964–1974 Decade* (New York: Academic Press, 1975), pp. 140–42. Also see George E. Rejda, "Social Security and the Paradox of the Welfare State," *Journal of Risk and Insurance*, vol. 39 (September 1972), pp. 17–39.

[8] In 1975, aggregate Consumer Population Survey (CPS) income was 90 percent of income estimated by independent sources, with the underreporting varying by source of income. Earnings from wages and salaries were almost entirely reported,

TABLE 28

PERCENTAGE DISTRIBUTION OF SOCIAL SECURITY BENEFICIARIES
AND SSI RECIPIENTS, BY INCOME, 1976

Income Group	Families, Head 65 and Over		Unrelated Aged Individuals	
	Social security[a]	SSI	Social security[a]	SSI
Loss–$1,999	—[b]	—[b]	8.5	14.6
$2,000–$2,999	3.0	—[b]	27.6	56.8
$3,000–$3,999	6.8	22.5	22.3	22.8
$4,000–$4,999	8.9	12.9	12.3	—[b]
$5,000–$6,999	19.3	21.3	13.7	—[b]
$7,000–$9,999	20.8	17.2	8.5	—[b]
$10,000 and over	40.2[c]	13.8	7.1	—[b]
All groups	100.0	100.0	100.0	100.0

NOTE: Persons as of March 1977.
[a] Includes railroad retirement income.
[b] Base is less than 75,000.
[c] About 19 percentage points are for families with $10,000–$14,999 and 21 points for those with $15,000 and over.
SOURCE: U.S. Bureau of the Census, unpublished data from the March 1976 *Consumer Population Survey*.

in the case of social security, would go to persons with incomes above the poverty threshold. For example, almost one-third of the aged family heads who reported receiving SSI in 1976 had annual incomes in excess of $7,000. Almost 13 percent of the aged families and 72 percent of unrelated aged individuals, however, reported gross incomes below $3,000. Consequently, increases in SSI payments, particularly to unrelated individuals, would do more to eradicate poverty than comparable increases in social security benefits.

The Relationship between Payroll Taxes and Benefits. The introduction of the SSI program increased the proportion of social security beneficiaries who also received welfare payments.[9] Dual recipiency

as compared with only 42 percent of dividend income. CPS data for SSI income and social security and railroad retirement benefits were 64 percent and 91 percent of the estimates from other sources. See U.S. Bureau of the Census, *Current Population Reports*, Series P-60, no. 106, "Money Income in 1975 of Families and Persons in the United States" (1977), p. 277.

[9] Between 1974 and 1977 the proportion of retirees whose monthly retirement benefit was below the SSI standard declined because the average social security retirement benefit increased at a faster rate than the SSI standards. For example,

improved the economic status of many aged and disabled persons, but combining social security benefits and SSI reduced the return that dual recipients received on their social security taxes. The maximum total social security tax paid by an employee and employer in 1977 was $1,930.50—a combined tax rate of 11.70 percent on a maximum taxable earnings of $16,500.[10] The tax rate was allocated in the following manner: 8.75 percentage points for old age and survivors insurance, 1.15 percentage points for disability insurance, and 1.80 percentage points for Medicare health insurance.

Retirement income. As was shown in Table 4, households receiving both social security benefits and SSI payments have a combined income only $20 larger than the SSI payment standards. For such households, there was frequently little relationship between the payroll taxes they paid and the combined benefits they received. In the middle of 1977, in states without supplementary payments, entitlement to social security benefits added only $20 to combined benefits when social security benefits were no greater than $198 for individuals and $287 for couples. The maximum social security cutoff points were higher in states making supplementary payments. In New York the amount was $259 for individuals and $363 for couples; in Wisconsin, $274 for individuals and $406 for couples; and in California, $316 for individuals and $577 for couples. In August 1977 the maximum social security benefit payable to a male retiring at age sixty-five at the beginning of 1977 was $413; the average benefit to retired workers was $255.[11]

Dual recipients receive only $20 of additional income for payroll taxes paid because of their entitlement to social security benefits. Evidently, this is a very low rate of return for many dual recipients.[12]

the federal SSI standard for an individual increased by 6.4 percent between December 1975 and December 1976, as compared with 8.7 percent for the average retirement benefit ($207 compared with $225). This difference reflects the fact that social security benefits increased in response to both a cost-of-living adjustment and the higher earnings of new beneficiaries, whereas the SSI standard increased only for the rise in the cost of living. Other things being equal, the incidence of dual beneficiaries would fall over time unless SSI benefits are indexed to the rate of increase in average retirement benefits instead of to the national increase in the consumer price index (CPI).

[10] The maximum combined tax in 1979 is $2,808, consisting of a combined tax rate of 12.26 percent on maximum taxable earnings of $22,900.

[11] See *Social Security Bulletin, Annual Statistical Supplement, 1975,* p. 25, and vol. 41 (April 1978), table M-13.

[12] Present retirees and those scheduled to retire in the near future are likely to be quite pleased with social security. A typical, low-earning male worker who retired at age sixty-five in 1976, for example, received an estimated annual real rate of

Similarly, social security beneficiaries whose benefits are above the SSI standards might equate the payoff with the difference between their social security check and the total SSI standard. Thus, a New York couple whose only other income in July 1977 was a social security benefit of $400 might feel that their payoff was only $57.

One way to improve the payoff for social security taxes for dual recipients and simultaneously to smooth the abrupt cutoff for SSI eligibility would be to increase the $20 disregard and scale the implicit tax rate of 100 percent on "excess" social security benefits. Table 29 shows what would have happened in December 1977 to the combined social security and SSI benefits of five individuals (A through E) with different social security pensions if the disregard was $20 and the tax rate ranged from 100 to 50 percent. The table assumes that no supplementary payments were made.

Example I shows the combined social security and SSI benefits under existing arrangements. Examples II to IV show the effect of lowering the tax rate from 100 percent to 50 percent. Each decrease raises the combined benefits of dual recipients and thus provides a larger payoff for social security taxes. Each decrease, however, adds more persons to the welfare rolls. At a tax rate of 50 percent, all five persons would receive SSI payments. The cost of the SSI program would be almost twice the cost at a tax rate of 100 percent ($480 versus $226).

Disability benefits. To qualify for social security disability insurance (DI) benefits, a worker must be unable to engage in any substantial gainful activity because of a medically determined physical or mental condition that is expected to last at least twelve continuous months or result in death.[13] In 1977 the disability had to be so severe that the person could not earn more than $230 a month in his usual type of work. In addition, a worker must have attained a disability-insured status. For a worker thirty-one years of age or older, this requires twenty quarters of coverage out of the last forty, ending with the quarter in which the disability occurs. A disabled person

---

return on his social security taxes ("investment") of 10 percent; his high-earning peer received 7.75 percent. Similarly, the estimated real rates of return for a male worker and his wife were 12 percent and 9.5 percent, respectively. See Alicia H. Munnell, *The Future of Social Security* (Washington, D.C.: Brookings Institution, 1977), table 3-5.

[13] Between 1960 and 1971 the proportion of disabled beneficiaries with earnings fluctuated between 5.7 percent and 11.4 percent. Median annual earnings were the highest ($665) in 1970. Paula Franklin, "Impact of Substantial Gainful Activity on Disabled Beneficiary Work Patterns," *Social Security Bulletin*, vol. 39 (August 1976), table 1.

TABLE 29

Four Examples of the Effects on Combined Social Security and
SSI Income from a $20 Income Disregard and Alternative
Tax Rates, December 1977
(dollars)

Four Examples/ Five Individuals with Different Social Security Benefits	Income Disregarded	SSI Income	Combined Social Security and SSI Income
Example I: $20 disregarded; 100 percent tax rate			
A. $ 0 benefit	20	178	178
B. $150 benefit	20	48	198
C. $200 benefit	0	0	200
D. $250 benefit	0	0	250
E. $300 benefit	0	0	300
Example II: $20 disregarded; 85 percent tax rate			
A. $ 0 benefit	20	178	178
B. $150 benefit	40	68	218
C. $200 benefit	47	25	225
D. $250 benefit	0	0	250
E. $300 benefit	0	0	300
Example III: $20 disregarded; 70 percent tax rate			
A. $ 0 benefit	20	178	178
B. $150 benefit	59	87	237
C. $200 benefit	74	52	252
D. $250 benefit	89	17	267
E. $300 benefit	0	0	300
Example IV: $20 disregarded; 50 percent tax rate			
A. $ 0 benefit	20	178	178
B. $150 benefit	85	113	263
C. $200 benefit	110	88	288
D. $250 benefit	135	63	313
E. $300 benefit	160	38	338

NOTE: Rounded to nearest dollar.

SOURCE: Author's calculations. The income disregarded equals $20 + (1 − tax rate) (social security benefit − $20).

must also satisfy a five-month waiting period before becoming entitled to disability benefits, which are related to the amount the worker would have been paid upon retiring at age sixty-five.

A significant number of disabled persons are ineligible for social security benefits, some because they fail the medical test, others because their earnings are too high, and some others because they do not have enough quarters of coverage. Disabled persons who do not satisfy DI criteria, as well as those with relatively low DI benefits, may qualify for SSI payments. In December 1977 about 35 percent of all disabled SSI recipients also had social security income, up markedly from 24 percent in December 1973. As with retirees, however, the expansion of welfare for the disabled has reduced the payoff for the disability portion of social security taxes.

In July 1977 the earnings criteria were different for SSI than for social security disability benefits. Since more earnings were disregarded by SSI than the $230 allowed by disability insurance, a disabled person could earn more under SSI than DI and still receive transfer income. During 1977 the SSI earnings disregard based only on the federal standard of $178 for individuals was $441, or $211 more than the social security DI exclusion.[14] The difference was even greater in states making supplementary payments. Furthermore, the difference will increase over time if the SSI standard ($178) and the DI exclusion ($230) increase at the same rate. If each increased 7 percent a year over the three-year period from July 1977 to July 1980, the substantial gainful activity requirement would reach $282 while the SSI ceiling would rise from $441 to $521.[15]

The SSI program has reduced the financial strain of the five-month waiting period for social security disability benefits. Since SSI does not have a waiting period and payments can be made based on presumed eligibility, disabled persons expected to qualify for SSI can receive some income while waiting for entitlement to DI benefits.

Medicare benefits. Most persons sixty-five years of age and over are eligible for Part A benefits of the Medicare program and, because of the 1972 amendments, disabled persons under sixty-five who receive DI benefits for at least twenty-four consecutive months are also eligible for these benefits. Part A covers major inpatient hospital and related posthospital services subject to certain deductibles, copayments, and limitations on the utilization of services. Aged and disabled persons can also enroll in Part B of the program for a monthly premium, which was about $9 a month in mid-1979. Part B covers physi-

---

[14] $441 = $85 + 2 ($178). For a discussion of the calculation, see Chapter 1.
[15] $282 = 230 (1.07)^3$; $521 = $85 + 2 (178) (1.07)^3$.

cian services, outpatient hospital care, home health services, and other medical services and supplies. The individual pays 20 percent of the reasonable charges for covered services after the annual deductible.

Medicare benefits are worth little to most SSI recipients because SSI recipients are automatically eligible for Medicaid—which provides more comprehensive coverage than Medicare. In most states, not only does Medicaid furnish some combination of outpatient prescriptions, false teeth and other dental care, eyeglasses, orthopedic shoes, and hearing aids, but it also provides significantly better protection against the cost of nursing home care. Also, Medicaid ordinarily pays the Medicare deductibles, copayments, and monthly Part B premiums. Hence, because of the superiority of Medicaid coverage, many social security beneficiaries would have had a greater aggregate income if they were not entitled to social security benefits. Under present law, however, SSI payments cannot be made to persons who fail to file for entitled social security benefits.

Minimum Benefit

The minimum social security benefit from 1939 to 1950 was $10 a month. Since then, the minimum has been increased at a faster rate than benefits in general, to $121 a month in 1978. The minimum benefit was initially designed for individuals who had low earnings and retired in the early years of the program. A worker retiring in 1977 could have qualified for the minimum benefit with twenty-four quarters of coverage.[16] About 565,000 persons who did not retire early received the minimum in December 1975, down from 739,000 in December 1972.[17] Many of these people, however, were not poor. This is because eligibility for the minimum benefit is not means-tested. Instead, it is paid to workers who accumulate sufficient time in covered employment regardless of their financial circumstances or their reason for spending little time in a covered occupation. Many people had relatively little covered time because they spent a significant portion of their working life in a noncovered occupation, such as federal employment.

---

[16] In 1972, the Congress added a special minimum benefit (SMB) for individuals who worked a lifetime at low wages. In 1977 the monthly SMB equaled $9 times the number of years (between ten and thirty) in covered employment, with a maximum of $180. The 1977 amendments raised the maximum to $230 as of 1979.

[17] *Social Security Bulletin, Annual Statistical Supplement, 1973 and 1975*, tables 78 and 87, respectively. In 1975 another 13,000 retirees received the minimum because of the reduction for early retirement, and another 1.2 million retirees received less than the minimum benefit.

Today, about 10 percent of all workers are not covered by social security. They consist primarily of federal government employees who are covered by the Civil Service Retirement System or state and local government employees. State and local governments can elect to enroll their employees in the OASDHI system. In March 1977, 72 percent of the 12.3 million state and local government employees were covered by social security, ranging from zero percent in Massachusetts to 100 percent in eleven states.[18]

Some persons whose primary occupation is not covered accumulate sufficient social security coverage either before or after working for the government or by working part-time at a second job. The earlier an individual retires from public service, the more likely he is to qualify for the minimum benefit. Uncovered retirees are encouraged to find another job since no reduction is made in a civil servant's public pension for social security benefits.[19]

In December 1975, about 44 percent of the 978,000 retired employees receiving a monthly pension under the federal Civil Service Retirement System received social security benefits, which roughly approximates the proportion of dual beneficiaries in 1967–1968.[20] Nearly 28 percent of the dual beneficiaries had a primary insurance amount at the minimum benefit level. (This amount is the base upon which social security benefits are computed but is not necessarily the amount paid.) About three-quarters of these people had at least twenty years of civil service employment. Most dual beneficiaries whose primary insurance amount was at the minimum benefit did not depend upon social security benefits for the bulk of their retirement income.[21] Only 2 percent had a civil service pension of less than $100; 10 percent, less than $200. In contrast, about 63 percent of the dual

---

[18] Social Security Administration, "Estimates of Covered State and Local Government Employment, March 31, 1977," *Research and Statistics Note*, note 7 (July 10, 1978), table 1.

[19] This is not true of 60 percent of private pension plans. In 1974 about one-quarter of the workers covered by these plans were denied some private pension benefits because of social security income.

[20] Elizabeth M. Heidbreder, "Federal Civil Service Annuitants and Social Security, 1975," *Social Security Bulletin*, vol. 40 (November 1977), pp. 3–4.

[21] In contrast, 53 percent of the federal pensioners whose primary insurance amount was greater than $299 received a monthly civil service annuity of less than $200. See ibid., table 9. For information on government pensions paid to dual beneficiaries in 1971, see Social Security Administration, *Income of the Population Aged 60 and Older, 1971*, Staff Paper no. 26 (April 1977). Table 8 shows that a government employee pension constituted less than half of the income of aged social security households. For 21 percent, the pension was less than one-fifth of their income.

beneficiaries had a monthly federal pension exceeding $400, including 9.1 percent with more than $899.[22]

A report prepared by the Social Security Administration concluded: "Any legislative change designed to eliminate such cases [dual pensioners] would give rise to inequities as between some of the people who would get reduced benefits and some who would get unreduced benefits."[23] The report also noted that the number of dual pensioners was smaller than might have been anticipated and would decline over time. A possible need to review the minimum benefit at some later point was, however, foreseen:

> We recommend against any legislative action to provide for reduction of social security benefits paid to Government employees. We suggest, however, that a broad approach, going beyond Government retirees, be considered if, at some future time, the Congress should contemplate very substantially raising the minimum benefits, say, to $100 or more. Provisions could then be considered that would assure that only people with reasonably long periods of covered work at low pay would receive the increased minimum benefits.[24]

The SSI program has eliminated the need for the minimum social security benefit. In July 1978 the federal SSI payment standard for an individual was 56 percent larger than the minimum benefit.[25] SSI would also have eventually eliminated the special minimum benefit if the 1977 amendments had not raised this benefit to $230 and linked future increases to automatic cost-of-living adjustments. Before these amendments, the special minimum benefit was no more than $180 (see note 16) and was not automatically adjusted for inflation. Since the federal SSI standard was $178 in July 1977, and since SSI payments increase automatically for cost-of-living increases, SSI would have completely eliminated the need for the special minimum benefit in 1978 if the 1977 changes were not made. In addition, SSI and the

[22] Heidbreder, "Federal Civil Service Annuitants and Social Security," table 9.

[23] Social Security Administration, *Relating Social Security Protection to the Federal Civil Service*, A Report Requested by the House Committee on Ways and Means and the Senate Committee on Finance (January 1969), pp. 38–39.

[24] Ibid., p. 39.

[25] There was widespread support to eliminate the minimum benefit. For example, see U.S. Congress, House of Representatives, *Reports of the Quadrennial Advisory Council on Social Security*, 94th Congress, 1st session, March 10, 1975, p. 37; *Report of the Consultant Panel on Social Security to the Congressional Research Service, Prepared for the Use of the Committee on Finance of the U.S. Senate and the Committee on Ways and Means of the U.S. House of Representatives*, 94th Congress, 2nd session, August 1976; and Munnell, *The Future of Social Security*, p. 52.

expansion of other means-tested programs have made it less necessary for the social security system to emphasize social adequacy at the expense of individual equity.

The 1977 amendments to the Social Security Act froze the minimum benefit at about $121. The freeze and the resulting gradual phaseout of the minimum benefit will relieve some of the financial pressure besetting the social security system.[26] Additional financial relief might be realized if SSI were used to eliminate welfare components of the social security program other than the minimum benefit. The Congress could then replace the progressive benefit structure with a proportional formula that would pay all retirees the same percentage of average monthly earnings. This would be an important step toward a system of social insurance in which all retirees receive an equitable return for their payroll taxes. With a proportionate tax structure, workers would be more inclined to perceive payroll taxes as savings rather than compulsory deductions from gross income, a perception that is important in sustaining political support for payroll taxes.

A proportionate tax structure would lead to a decline in the amount of social security benefits paid to persons with low incomes and a rise in SSI payments. It would also subject a larger number of people to a means test. If the number of elderly persons with SSI doubled, roughly 20 percent of the elderly would have to undergo this unpopular and often resented test. Political pressure might develop to avoid this situation and to prevent additional people from incurring the stigma of being labeled welfare recipients.

If the welfare components of the social security system were eliminated, certain aspects of the SSI program would have to be revised. Resource limitations would have to be modified to coincide with the financial status of the new recipients. Current SSI limitations on savings and the value of automobiles, for example, would have to be modified to recognize differences between the amount of wealth held by SSI recipients and social security beneficiaries. The SSI earnings test would have to be coordinated with the social security retirement test, which is described below. The minimum age for elderly SSI

---

[26] In 1977 the Congress passed hefty increases in social security taxes to resolve some of the financial problems. The increases are scheduled to go into effect between 1978 and 1990. For an analysis of the 1977 legislation, see Colin D. Campbell, *The 1977 Amendments to the Social Security Act* (Washington, D.C.: American Enterprise Institute, 1978); John Snee and Mary Ross, "Social Security Amendments of 1977: Legislative History and Summary of Provisions," *Social Security Bulletin*, vol. 41 (March 1978), pp. 3–20; and A. Haeworth Robertson, "Financial Status of Social Security Program after the Social Security Amendments of 1977," *Social Security Bulletin*, vol. 41 (March 1978), pp. 21–30.

recipients would have to be lowered to sixty-two to accommodate early retirees. Rules and regulations would have to be established concerning state supplements and the intergovernmental sharing of additional SSI payments. Although there would be substantial problems of implementation, the gains from strengthening the social security system might justify the costs.

Additional general tax revenues would be needed if the Congress decided to shift the funding responsibility for social security's welfare components.[27] These revenues could be raised by increasing federal taxes at the same time social security taxes are lowered. The net impact of these changes would vary among taxpayers. Lower-income persons would be net gainers since the decrease in their social security taxes would be greater than the increase in their federal income taxes. Conversely, higher-income persons would lose out since the increase in their federal taxes would outweigh the decline in their social security taxes.

Inducements to Retire

Because of the retirement test, the benefits of persons that are eligible for social security may be reduced if they continue in gainful employment.[28] Although this test now applies to all persons under age seventy-two, in 1982 it will apply only to persons under age seventy. In 1977, for persons aged sixty-five and over, retirement benefits were reduced by $1 for every $2 of earnings in excess of $3,000.[29] In 1979 workers aged sixty-five to seventy-two are able to earn $4,500 before starting to lose benefits. Proponents of the test ordinarily justify it on three grounds: to avoid paying social security to persons who have not lost earnings; to increase job opportunities for younger people by encouraging older persons to retire; and to avoid increasing the cost of the social security program. Opponents of the test argue that it discourages the elderly from participating in the labor force, is dis-

---

[27] A shift in funding differs materially from using general taxes to bolster social security. A general revenue contribution from the Treasury to the social security trust funds, regularly or periodically, implies that the social security system is financially unsound. A law requiring the transfer of welfare components to the Treasury does not. Rather, it suggests that a portion of the present social security system will be financed by a more appropriate tax base.

[28] The concept of retirement is not unambiguous. Some relate to it to (1) the receipt of a pension, regardless of work status; (2) the cessation or reduction of work or earnings from a lifetime career; or (3) an individual's perception of his retirement status.

[29] In 1975 male retirees with reduced benefits averaged $207 per month, as compared with $247 for men without a reduction. See *Social Security Bulletin, Annual Statistical Supplement, 1975*, table 95.

criminatory compared with retirement plans that do not penalize retirees for working, and treats income from earnings differently from other forms of income, regardless of need.[30]

Both the social security and the SSI earnings tests limit the amount that can be earned without a reduction in benefits and have an implicit tax rate of 50 percent on earnings above a fixed amount. The tests differ with respect to the amount of income disregarded and the testing period. Considerably more retirement income is allowed by the social security system than the SSI program. In 1977 SSI disregarded the first $65 ($85 in the absence of unearned income) of monthly earnings, as compared with the first $250 under social security. The SSI test was applied quarterly; the social security test was annual with the proviso that benefits were payable in any month during which earnings were less than the $250 exclusion.

It was almost impossible for individuals to lose social security benefits because of the retirement test and still qualify for SSI. This can be illustrated by comparing the level of earnings at which individuals no longer qualify for benefits under each program separately. If the flat disregards are expressed on a monthly basis, the break-even amount can be calculated by multiplying the payment amount by the reciprocal of the implicit tax rate and adding the result to the flat exclusion or disregard. To illustrate, for July 1977,

Maximum earnings under OAI = $250 + 2 (OAI benefits)

Maximum earnings under SSI = $85 + 2 (SSI standard).

These equations suggest that, if the SSI payment standard equaled the social security benefit, break-even earnings for social security benefits were $165 greater than break-even earnings for SSI payments. The difference in break-even earnings narrowed if the SSI standard exceeded the social security benefit. If the SSI standard exceeded the benefit by half the difference in the flat disregard (here $82.50), the break-even levels would be identical. Theoretically, if the SSI standard exceeded the social security benefit by a larger amount, an individual could have been ineligible for social security but still qualified for SSI. This was not likely to have happened in 1977; if it did, it probably occurred in instances where a person had a relatively low retirement

---

[30] In 1971 only 19 percent of all retired workers aged sixty-two to seventy-one were affected by the retirement test. However, the test's impact on retired-worker beneficiaries was considerable—a loss of 71 percent of the $3.1 billion in benefits they otherwise were entitled to receive. See Barbara A. Lingg, "Retired-Worker Beneficiaries Affected by the Annual Earnings Test in 1971," *Social Security Bulletin*, vol. 38 (August 1975), pp. 23–25. Grad reports that the retirement decision is highly stable; few workers awarded benefits are likely to have benefits suspended later because of work. See Susan Grad, "New Retirees and the Stability of the Retirement Decision," *Social Security Bulletin*, vol. 40 (March 1977), pp. 7–8.

benefit and resided in a state making relatively generous SSI supplementary payments. It is less likely to happen in the future because of the scheduled rapid growth in the amount of earnings disregarded by social security.

A male worker may elect to retire at age sixty-two but will receive a permanently reduced social security benefit equal to five-ninths of 1 percent for each month he retires before age sixty-five. The pension of a person retiring at age sixty-two is 80 percent of the amount he would have received if he continued working to sixty-five. Between 1960 and 1975, the proportion of beneficiaries with reduced benefits because of early retirement rose from 11.8 percent to 56.5 percent.

Individuals retire for a variety of reasons. Surveys by the Social Security Administration have concluded that many people retire involuntarily because of ill health, union pressures, economic discrimination, and discouragement stemming from the difficulty of finding a new job or retraining to keep up with technological advance. A growing proportion of persons appear to be retiring before age sixty-five because they prefer the leisure of retirement. Initial findings of the Social Security Administration Retirement History Study show that, in 1973, 30 percent of the males who worked in 1969 and were aged sixty-two and sixty-three and 36 percent of those aged sixty-four and sixty-five left their jobs to draw a pension, work less, or change jobs and not because of poor health.[31] Increased preference for retirement is also suggested by the decline in labor force participation rates for older males. About 46 percent of the men sixty-five and over were in the labor force in 1950, as compared with 21.7 percent in 1975; the participation rate for men aged sixty to sixty-four dipped from 78 percent in 1950 to 65.7 percent in 1975. Moreover, the Bureau of Labor Statistics estimates that in 1990 these rates will decline to 16.8 percent and 57.7 percent, respectively.[32]

Voluntary and early retirement have been made increasingly possible by the growth of public and private pensions, particularly social security benefits. There is a lack of consensus, however, on how strong the influence of social security is on retirement.[33] In general, researchers outside the Social Security Administration have concluded that its influence is more important than has been indicated by the

---

[31] Lenore E. Bixby, "Retirement Patterns in the United States: Research and Policy Interaction," *Social Security Bulletin*, vol. 39 (August 1976), table 8.

[32] U.S. Bureau of Labor Statistics, *New Labor Force Projections to 1990*, Special Labor Force Report no. 197 (1977), p. A-2.

[33] For a review of these studies, see Colin D. Campbell and Rosemary G. Campbell, "Conflicting Views on the Effect of Old Age and Survivors Insurance on Retirement," *Economic Inquiry*, vol. 14 (September 1976), pp. 369–88.

administration's researchers. In part, this difference may be because the Social Security Administration uses the interview technique to obtain information. People may feel it is socially unacceptable to admit they retired because of the availability of social security or a desire to stop working. Another possibility is that Social Security Administration researchers hesitate to "blame OASI for a decline in labor force participation of elderly persons, but would be expected to want to promote the organization in which they are employed."[34]

SSI may encourage certain people to retire early if at age sixty-five the reduction in their social security benefits because of early retirement is offset by their SSI payments. The inducement is likely to be strongest among wage earners who are already inclined toward early retirement and reside in states with high supplementary standards. Consider the case of a man who retired at age sixty-two on July 1, 1975, who otherwise would have received a social security benefit of $280 at age sixty-five. Early retirement lowers his benefit by $56 to $224. If he had no other income and satisfied all other eligibility criteria, three years later he would receive an SSI supplement of about $38 if he resided in California or Massachusetts. The difference of $18 ($56 — $38) could easily be offset by the value of the Medicaid and other in-kind transfers that SSI recipients are eligible to receive. Such persons might be better off today, therefore, if they had retired at age sixty-two rather than age sixty-five.

---

[34] Ibid., p. 386.

CONCLUSION

In August 1977 President Carter released the details of his initial proposal for welfare reform; he recommended that the Supplemental Security Income, Assistance to Families with Dependent Children, General Assistance, Emergency Assistance, and food stamp programs be replaced by the Program for Better Jobs and Income (PBJI). Essentially, the new program was to represent "the largest jobs program since the Great Depression with a program of cash assistance for the poor that is fairer and simpler than the hodge-podge that exists now."[1]

In May 1979 the President sent to Congress a scaled-down, noticeably less ambitious program for welfare reform as explained in two bills: the Welfare Reform Amendments of 1979 and the Work Training Opportunities Act of 1979. Unlike the original package, the new proposal does not sponsor the consolidation of existing welfare programs into one superfederal program. Instead, it focuses on establishing a national minimum payment standard for AFDC families along the lines of the SSI program, and furnishing work training and jobs for low income families. Scant references are made to the SSI program.

The PBJI was expected to increase both the payments to, and the number of, aged, blind, and disabled recipients above the levels they would have reached otherwise because of an increase in standards and a liberalization of income disregards and resource limitations. In addition to allowing the aged, blind, and disabled to own a home and still receive welfare, the administration's 1977 proposal would have al-

---

[1] U.S. Department of Health, Education, and Welfare, "Welfare Reform," *HEW News*, August 6, 1977; and *New York Times*, August 7, 1977, pp. 1, 40–41. An analysis of the original proposal is in Congressional Budget Office, *The Administration's Welfare Reform Proposal: An Analysis of the Program for Better Jobs and Income* (April 1978).

lowed them to own household and personal effects of any value and still qualify for welfare. Further, the value of an automobile excluded in determining eligibility would have risen to $3,000 and individuals could have excluded the value of a prepaid burial contract of any value. The new legislation does not propose these changes.

The Welfare Reform Amendments support a merging of the SSI and food stamp programs for certain SSI recipients. Today about 40 percent of the 3.3 million SSI recipients living outside the three cash-out states receive food stamps. About 500,000 of those not receiving stamps do not qualify for them because they either reside with persons ineligible for food stamps or reside in an institution. The remainder, according to the administration, do not participate in the program "presumably because they are ignorant of their availability or because of the hassle of applying or the stigma of using the stamps in stores."[2]

The administration proposes to cash out food stamps for recipients not living in larger households.[3] An additional payment would be made monthly to all recipients of a federal payment and persons receiving only state supplementary payments if these payments are federally administered. Recipients who would be hurt financially by the cash out will be grandfathered into the new program at the bonus value of their food stamps. The cash out is expected to benefit about 1.3 million persons at a gross federal cost of $625 million in 1982, including the cost of the grandfathered recipients. Gross costs are expected to be reduced by $222 million from the contraction of the present food stamp program, for a net increase of $403 million.[4]

As in the case of the SSI program, administrative efficiency and fiscal relief for the states are major selling points for welfare reform. The administration estimates that in 1982 its program will save the states about $1.1 billion. California is expected to save $222 million, followed by Illinois ($152 million), New York ($145 million), and Massachusetts ($104 million).[5] These estimates do not reflect the equivalent of optional SSI supplements, nor do they include the possi-

---

[2] President Carter's Proposal for Welfare Reform, *Work and Training Opportunities Act of 1979 and the Social Welfare Reform Amendments of 1979* (May 23, 1979), p. 32.

[3] Food stamps will not be cashed out for SSI recipients who are members of larger households because their eligibility for the stamps depends on the financial status of the larger household. Also, the substitution of cash for stamps might be costly if the cash out is paid to SSI recipients ineligible for food stamps, and the cash out for an SSI recipient increases the value of the stamp benefit to other household members.

[4] President Carter's Proposal for Welfare Reform, p. 63.

[5] Ibid., table III, p. 54.

ble effects of welfare reform on Medicaid payments. Moreover, the new program will result in a net increase in taxes since the states' fiscal relief will be more than offset by an increase in federal taxes.

The administration's proposal for welfare reform has been developed independently of the social security system. To the extent the President's plan expands welfare for the aged, blind, and disabled, it will accentuate the overlapping of social security, SSI, and other welfare programs. For a growing number of people, welfare will be preferable to social security benefits either because welfare payments will be higher than social security benefits or because eligibility for cash assistance will enable welfare recipients to have a higher cash and in-kind income than nonrecipients.

Implementation of the administration's program will heighten the need to define more clearly the purposes and goals of social security and to integrate social security with SSI and other welfare programs. Lack of coordination is likely to affect adversely the public's acceptance of the social security program and to aggravate inequities. Making the social security benefit structure more strictly wage-related and letting SSI and other welfare programs address questions of poverty and minimum income is one way to rationalize these programs. Social security is not an efficient way to combat poverty nor is a payroll-financed retirement plan an equitable way to redistribute income to needy persons.

APPENDIX

TABLE A-1

ADMINISTRATION OF THE SSI STATE SUPPLEMENTARY PROGRAMS AND THE
DETERMINATION OF MEDICAID ELIGIBILITY, JULY 1, 1978

	Administration		Medicaid Eligibility	
Region/State	Mandatory	Optional	Standard	Deter-mination
Region I				
Connecticut	State	State	January 1972	State
Maine	Federal	Federal	Title XVI	SSA
Massachusetts	Federal	Federal	Title XVI	SSA
New Hampshire	State	State	January 1972	State
Rhode Island	Federal	Federal	Title XVI	SSA
Vermont	Federal	Federal	Title XVI	SSA
Region II				
New Jersey	Federal	Federal	Title XVI	SSA
New York	Federal	Federal	Title XVI	SSA
Region III				
Delaware	Federal	Federal	Title XVI	SSA
District of Columbia	Federal	Federal	Title XVI	SSA
Maryland	Federal	State	Title XVI	SSA
Pennsylvania	Federal	Federal	Title XVI	SSA
Virginia	State	State	January 1972	State
West Virginia	None	None	Title XVI	SSA
Region IV				
Alabama	State	State	Title XVI	SSA
Florida	Federal	State	Title XVI	SSA
Georgia	Federal	None	Title XVI	SSA
Kentucky	State	State	Title XVI	SSA
Mississippi	Federal	None	January 1972	State
North Carolina	State	State	January 1972	State
South Carolina	State	State	Title XVI	SSA
Tennessee	Federal	None	Title XVI	SSA
Region V				
Illinois	State	State	January 1972	State
Indiana	State	State	January 1972	State
Michigan	Federal	Federal	Title XVI	SSA
Minnesota	State	State	January 1972	State
Ohio	Federal	State	January 1972	State
Wisconsin	Federal	Federal	Title XVI	SSA
Region VI				
Arkansas	Federal	None	Title XVI	SSA
Louisiana	Federal	None	Title XVI	SSA
New Mexico	State	State	Title XVI	SSA

Region/State	Administration		Medicaid Eligibility	
	Mandatory	Optional	Standard	Determination
Oklahoma	State	State	January 1972	State
Texas	None	None	Title XVI	SSA
Region VII				
Iowa	Federal	Federal	Title XVI	SSA
Kansas	Federal	None	Title XVI	State
Missouri	State	State	January 1972	State
Nebraska	State	State	January 1972	State
Region VIII				
Arizona	State	State	a	a
Colorado	State	State	Title XVI	State
Montana	Federal	Federal	Title XVI	SSA
North Dakota	State	State	Title XVI	State
South Dakota	Federal	State	Title XVI	SSA
Utah	State	State	January 1972	State
Wyoming	State	State	Title XVI	SSA
Region IX				
California	Federal	Federal	Title XVI	SSA
Hawaii	Federal	Federal	January 1972	State
Nevada	Federal	Federal	Title XVI	State
Region X				
Alaska	State	State	Title XVI	State
Idaho	State	State	Title XVI	State
Oregon	State	State	Title XVI	State
Washington	Federal	Federal	Title XVI	SSA

a No Medicaid program.

SOURCE: Social Security Administration, *Supplemental Security Income for the Aged, Blind, and Disabled: Summary of State Payment Levels, State Supplementation and Medicaid Decisions* (October 1, 1978).

TABLE A-2

NUMBER OF AGED, BLIND, AND DISABLED RECIPIENTS IN DECEMBER 1973 AND DECEMBER 1977
(thousands)

Region/State	Aged Recipients			Disabled Recipients			Total Aged, Blind, and Disabled Recipients		
	1973	1977ᵃ	Percent change	1973	1977ᵃ	Percent change	1973	1977ᵃ	Percent change
United States	1,800.8	2,078.0	15.4	1,257.9	2,131.7	69.5	3,135.5	4,287.7	36.8
Region I									
Connecticut	7.0	10.1	44.3	10.7	18.2	70.1	17.9	28.7	60.3
Maine	11.8	11.5	− 2.5	7.7	11.1	44.2	19.8	22.9	15.7
Massachusetts	57.3	74.2	29.5	29.7	50.7	70.7	89.9	129.7	44.3
New Hampshire	4.4	2.5	−43.2	1.5	2.8	86.7	6.2	5.5	−11.3
Rhode Island	3.8	6.5	71.1	5.7	8.9	56.1	9.6	15.6	62.5
Vermont	3.9	4.1	5.1	2.8	4.7	67.9	6.8	9.0	32.4
Total	88.2	108.9	23.5	58.1	96.4	65.9	150.2	211.4	40.7
Region II									
New Jersey	20.5	34.3	67.3	22.1	45.3	105.0	43.5	80.6	85.3
New York	106.3	154.5	45.3	174.5	225.2	29.1	285.1	383.6	34.5
Total	126.8	188.8	48.9	196.6	270.5	37.6	328.6	464.2	41.3
Region III									
Delaware	2.9	2.9	0.0	2.1	4.0	90.5	5.3	7.1	34.0
District of Columbia	4.2	4.6	9.5	10.5	10.0	− 4.8	14.9	14.8	− 0.7
Maryland	10.3	17.7	71.8	26.4	30.1	14.0	37.1	48.4	30.5

Pennsylvania	37.0	66.2	78.9	47.3	97.8	106.8	90.1	167.8	86.2
Virginia	14.0	39.1	179.3	13.3	38.5	189.5	28.6	79.1	176.6
West Virginia	11.3	17.2	52.2	12.0	25.1	109.2	23.9	42.9	79.5
Total	79.7	147.7	85.3	111.6	205.5	84.1	199.9	360.1	80.1
Region IV									
Alabama	106.3	92.5	−13.0	21.0	51.4	144.8	129.3	145.8	12.8
Florida	67.3	88.4	31.4	24.9	73.5	195.2	94.4	164.5	74.3
Georgia	81.7	82.2	0.6	40.4	75.5	86.9	125.2	160.6	28.3
Kentucky	51.4	49.8	− 3.1	19.9	44.1	121.6	73.4	95.9	30.7
Mississippi	80.6	71.2	−11.7	28.5	45.2	58.6	111.1	118.2	6.4
North Carolina	30.9	72.3	134.0	36.2	70.4	94.5	71.6	146.3	104.3
South Carolina	17.5	42.6	143.4	14.5	38.7	166.9	33.9	83.2	145.4
Tennessee	45.4	69.7	53.5	31.5	62.6	98.7	78.5	134.1	70.8
Total	481.1	568.7	18.2	216.9	461.4	112.7	717.4	1,048.6	46.2
Region V									
Illinois	31.0	42.9	38.4	83.8	93.3	11.3	116.4	137.8	18.4
Indiana	13.4	18.2	35.8	11.1	21.9	97.3	25.8	41.1	59.3
Michigan	37.9	44.7	17.9	53.7	71.1	32.4	93.3	117.4	25.8
Minnesota	12.3	16.0	30.1	14.7	19.4	32.0	27.8	36.0	29.5
Ohio	42.9	44.3	3.3	51.1	79.9	56.4	96.3	126.6	31.5
Wisconsin	13.5	33.6	148.9	9.9	32.5	228.3	24.1	67.0	178.0
Total	151.0	199.7	32.3	224.3	318.1	41.8	383.7	525.9	37.1
Region VI									
Arkansas	56.7	50.7	−10.6	13.8	32.0	131.9	72.2	84.3	16.8
Louisiana	101.8	80.0	−21.4	24.9	65.9	164.7	128.7	148.1	15.1
New Mexico	7.5	11.4	52.0	10.5	14.0	33.3	18.4	25.8	40.2
Oklahoma	50.3	45.2	−10.1	22.2	33.8	52.3	73.5	80.1	9.0
Texas	169.9	169.1	− 0.5	31.3	100.2	220.1	205.0	273.3	33.3
Total	386.2	356.4	− 7.7	102.7	245.9	139.4	497.8	611.6	22.9

TABLE A-2—Continued

Region/State	Aged Recipients			Disabled Recipients			Total Aged, Blind, and Disabled Recipients		
	1973	1977[a]	Percent change	1973	1977[a]	Percent change	1973	1977[a]	Percent change
Region VII									
Iowa	10.9	13.3	22.0	3.6	12.5	247.2	15.5	27.0	74.2
Kansas	8.5	10.3	21.2	7.3	11.9	63.0	16.1	22.5	39.8
Missouri	88.9	59.1	−33.5	25.3	40.9	61.7	118.3	102.2	−13.6
Nebraska	6.3	7.5	19.0	6.3	8.1	28.6	12.9	15.8	22.5
Total	114.6	90.2	−21.3	42.5	73.4	72.7	162.8	167.5	2.9
Region VIII									
Arizona	12.8	13.1	2.3	10.3	15.3	48.5	23.5	28.9	23.0
Colorado	25.9	21.8	−15.8	13.7	18.6	35.8	39.7	40.7	2.5
Montana	2.6	2.9	11.5	3.2	4.5	40.6	5.9	7.5	27.1
North Dakota	3.2	4.0	25.0	2.0	3.1	55.0	5.3	7.2	35.8
South Dakota	3.1	4.4	41.9	2.0	3.7	85.0	5.2	8.3	59.6
Utah	3.9	2.9	−25.6	5.7	5.4	− 5.3	9.8	8.4	−14.3
Wyoming	1.2	1.1	− 8.3	1.1	1.1	0.0	2.3	2.2	− 4.3
Total	52.7	50.2	− 4.7	38.0	51.7	36.1	91.7	103.2	12.5
Region IX									
California	285.8	325.6	13.9	218.6	349.9	60.1	518.5	692.6	33.6
Hawaii	3.2	5.3	65.6	2.8	4.6	64.3	6.1	9.9	62.3
Nevada	2.2	3.5	59.1	—[b]	2.2	—	2.3	6.0	160.9
Total	291.2	334.4	14.8	221.4	356.7	61.1	526.9	708.5	34.5

Region X									
Alaska	2.1	1.5	−28.6	1.7	1.9	11.8	3.8	3.5	—
Idaho	3.0	3.2	6.7	3.3	4.5	36.4	6.4	7.9	23.4
Oregon	7.6	10.0	31.6	11.0	15.3	39.1	19.3	26.0	34.7
Washington	16.6	18.3	10.2	29.8	30.4	2.0	46.8	49.1	4.9
Total	29.3	33.0	12.6	45.8	52.1	13.8	76.3	86.5	13.4

NOTE: Detail may not add because of rounding.

a Partly estimated. Includes persons with federal SSI payments, federally administered state supplements, or state-administered state supplements.

b No program.

SOURCES: Social Security Bulletin (June 1974), table M-27; and Supplemental Security Income for the Aged, Blind, and Disabled, Monthly Statistics (December 1977), table 4, and (February 1978), table 12.

TABLE A-3

AGED RECIPIENTS: RECIPIENT RATE, AVERAGE MONTHLY PAYMENT PER RECIPIENT, AND ANNUAL PER CAPITA EXPENDITURE PER PERSON AGED SIXTY-FIVE AND OVER, 1973 AND 1977

Region/State	Recipient Rate		Average Monthly Payment per Recipient (dollars)		Annual per Capita Expenditure per Person 65 and Over (dollars)	
	1973	1977[a]	1973	1977[a]	1973	1977[a]
United States	85	90	80	97	82	104
Region I						
Connecticut	23	30	97	93	27	33
Maine	96	90	75	60	87	65
Massachusetts	87	107	109	115	114	148
New Hampshire	52	28	112	87	70	30
Rhode Island	35	55	73	76	30	50
Vermont	79	75	75	92	71	83
Average for Region	66	76	100	103	80	95
Region II						
New Jersey	26	43	82	95	26	49
New York	55	74	101	110	66	99
Average for Region	47	66	98	108	55	85
Region III						
Delaware	64	55	86	75	66	50

District of Columbia	56	66	99	90	66	71
Maryland	30	50	68	78	25	47
Pennsylvania	28	46	74	98	25	54
Virginia	34	88	78	74	32	79
West Virginia	57	80	97	85	66	81
Average for Region	33	58	79	87	32	60
Region IV						
Alabama	303	237	74	86	269	245
Florida	57	61	83	97	56	71
Georgia	207	184	59	82	145	182
Kentucky	148	138	69	92	122	153
Mississippi	336	275	55	84	222	276
North Carolina	66	140	80	85	64	143
South Carolina	82	175	57	78	56	164
Tennessee	110	155	55	77	73	143
Average for Region	133	139	67	86	107	143
Region V						
Illinois	28	37	70	85	24	37
Indiana	27	34	58	68	19	28
Michigan	49	53	72	102	42	65
Minnesota	29	36	66	74	23	32
Ohio	42	41	63	77	32	38
Wisconsin	39	64	113	94	53	72
Average for Region	36	43	72	86	32	45
Region VI						
Arkansas	219	184	69	77	181	169
Louisiana	314	227	74	88	280	240

TABLE A-3—Continued

Region/State	Recipient Rate		Average Monthly Payment per Recipient (dollars)		Annual per Capita Expenditure per Person 65 and Over (dollars)	
	1973	1977[a]	1973	1977[a]	1973	1977[a]
New Mexico	93	119	57	82	63	117
Oklahoma	162	134	68	110	132	176
Texas	158	140	55	78	105	131
Average for Region	188	157	64	84	145	159
Region VII						
Iowa	31	37	71	66	27	29
Kansas	31	36	63	71	23	31
Missouri	153	99	84	87	154	104
Nebraska	35	38	65	76	27	35
Average for Region	82	63	80	81	79	62
Region VIII						
Arizona	64	54	80	96	62	62
Colorado	131	100	78	97	122	117
Montana	35	39	63	68	27	32
North Dakota	54	54	92	73	60	48
South Dakota	38	54	65	74	30	48
Utah	25	31	80	82	23	30
Wyoming	36	31	66	73	29	27
Average for Region	70	73	78	75	65	66

Region IX						
California	149	149	112	138	200	246
Hawaii	61	83	107	113	79	112
Nevada	71	68	74	94	63	77
Average for Region	145	145	112	137	194	239
Region X						
Alaska	255	167	119	183	364	366
Idaho	41	40	71	92	35	45
Oregon	29	37	80	78	28	35
Washington	48	46	77	94	45	52
Average for Region	43	44	80	92	42	48

ᵃ Partly estimated.

SOURCES: Numbers of recipients for July 1973 from *Social Security Bulletin*, vol. 36 (December 1973), table M-27; and Social Security Administration, *Supplemental Security Income for the Aged, Blind, and Disabled, Monthly Statistics* (July 1977) and (September 1978), tables 4 and 12, respectively. Payment data from *Social Security Bulletin, Annual Statistical Supplement, 1973*, table 145, and unpublished data provided by the Social Security Administration. Population data from U.S. Bureau of the Census, *Current Population Reports*, Series P-25, no. 734.

TABLE A-4

Disabled Recipients: Recipient Rate, Average Monthly Payment per Recipient, and Annual per Capita Expenditure per Person Aged Eighteen to Sixty-Four Years, 1973 and 1977

Region/State	Recipient Rate		Average Monthly Payment per Recipient		Annual per Capita Expenditure per Person 18-64 Years	
	1973	1977[a]	1973	1977[a]	1973	1977[a]
United States	10.0	16.3	112	148	13	29
Region I						
Connecticut	5.8	9.3	130	136	9	15
Maine	11.9	17.5	108	113	15	24
Massachusetts	8.4	14.2	152	177	15	30
New Hampshire	3.1	5.2	124	180	5	11
Rhode Island	9.3	15.9	111	130	12	25
Vermont	10.3	15.8	117	143	15	27
Average for Region	7.8	12.8	136	156	13	24
Region II						
New Jersey	4.9	10.0	112	142	7	17
New York	15.3	20.5	147	173	27	43
Average for Region	12.3	17.5	144	168	21	35
Region III						
Delaware	6.2	10.2	113	132	8	16

District of Columbia	22.0	23.1	122	145	32	40
Maryland	8.4	11.6	97	135	10	19
Pennsylvania	6.2	13.3	95	154	7	25
Virginia	4.5	11.7	98	119	5	17
West Virginia	11.5	22.3	90	134	12	36
Average for Region	7.1	13.6	98	141	8	23
Region IV						
Alabama	10.1	23.4	80	120	10	34
Florida	5.7	14.8	92	128	6	23
Georgia	14.7	24.5	69	117	12	34
Kentucky	10.2	21.6	94	132	12	34
Mississippi	22.7	34.1	65	125	18	51
North Carolina	10.7	20.8	86	127	11	32
South Carolina	8.8	22.0	67	120	7	32
Tennessee	13.0	23.8	74	122	11	35
Average for Region	11.0	21.6	78	124	10	32
Region V						
Illinois	13.7	14.2	107	137	18	23
Indiana	3.7	6.8	59	111	3	9
Michigan	9.9	12.8	116	154	14	24
Minnesota	6.6	8.3	96	109	8	11
Ohio	7.9	12.4	87	128	8	19
Wisconsin	3.9	11.7	117	146	6	20
Average for Region	8.7	11.8	102	136	11	19
Region VI						
Arkansas	11.8	25.8	83	108	12	33
Louisiana	11.3	28.5	60	124	8	42

TABLE A-4—Continued

Region/State	Recipient Rate		Average Monthly Payment per Recipient		Annual per Capita Expenditure per Person 18-64 Years	
	1973	1977[a]	1973	1977[a]	1973	1977[a]
New Mexico	16.4	20.3	78	127	15	31
Oklahoma	14.4	20.5	102	131	18	32
Texas	4.3	12.8	75	113	4	17
Average for Region	8.1	17.9	79	119	8	26
Region VII						
Iowa	2.0	7.5	96	104	2	9
Kansas	5.1	8.5	81	103	5	11
Missouri	9.0	14.3	87	123	9	21
Nebraska	7.3	8.6	101	130	9	13
Average for Region	6.3	10.7	89	117	7	15
Region VIII						
Arizona	8.9	11.5	89	136	10	19
Colorado	8.8	11.3	90	145	10	20
Montana	7.2	10.3	97	123	8	15
North Dakota	5.6	8.3	110	121	7	12
South Dakota	5.0	9.5	81	109	5	12
Utah	8.7	7.6	85	114	9	10
Wyoming	4.6	4.5	83	110	5	6
Average for Region	7.9	10.1	90	132	9	16
Region IX						
California	17.3	25.8	149	204	30	63

Hawaii	5.1	7.5	146	161	9	14
Nevada	—[b]	5.6	—[b]	123	—[b]	8
Average for Region	16.4	24.6	149	204	29	60
Region X						
Alaska	8.0	7.8	171	215	16	20
Idaho	7.7	9.1	96	140	9	15
Oregon	7.5	10.8	103	129	9	17
Washington	13.7	13.4	119	153	20	25
Average for Region	10.7	11.8	115	147	15	21

[a] Partly estimated.

[b] No program.

SOURCES: Numbers of recipients for July 1973 from *Social Security Bulletin*, vol. 36 (December 1973), table M-27; and *Social Security Administration, Supplemental Security Income for the Aged, Blind, and Disabled, Monthly Statistics* (July 1977) and (September 1978), tables 4 and 12, respectively. Payment data from *Social Security Bulletin, Annual Statistical Supplement, 1973*, table 145, and unpublished data provided by the Social Security Administration. Population data from U.S. Bureau of the Census, *Current Population Reports*, Series P-25, no. 734.

TABLE A-5

PUBLIC ASSISTANCE AND SSI PAYMENTS TO AGED, BLIND, AND DISABLED RECIPIENTS, 1973 AND 1977

(millions of dollars)

Region/State	Payments to Aged Recipients			Payments to Disabled Recipients			Total Payments to Aged, Blind, and Disabled Recipients		
	1973	1977[a]	Percent change	1973	1977[a]	Percent change	1973	1977[a]	Percent change
United States	1,738.6	2,448.3[b]	42.3	1,606.5	3,709.5[b]	130.9	3,449.6	6,304.3[b]	83.5
Region I									
Connecticut	8.2	11.3	37.8	16.2	28.6	76.5	24.8	40.4	62.9
Maine	10.4	8.4	−19.2	8.8	14.9	69.3	19.6	23.7	20.9
Massachusetts	74.3	101.5	36.6	50.8	104.7	106.1	130.4	217.1	66.5
New Hampshire	5.8	2.8	−51.7	2.1	5.6	166.7	8.3	8.7	4.8
Rhode Island	3.3	5.9	78.8	7.0	13.8	97.1	10.5	20.0	90.5
Vermont	3.6	4.5	25.0	3.8	7.7	102.6	7.5	12.4	65.3
Total	105.6	134.4	27.3	88.7	175.3	97.6	201.1	322.3	60.3
Region II									
New Jersey	19.0	39.5	107.9	28.0	75.6	170.0	48.2	116.7	142.1
New York	131.6	205.3	56.0	289.0	459.3	58.9	427.1	672.4	57.4
Total	150.6	244.8	62.5	317.0	534.9	68.7	475.3	789.1	66.0

Region III								
Delaware	3.1	2.6	−16.1	2.8	5.7	103.6	6.3	8.6	36.5
District of Columbia	4.7	5.0	6.4	14.5	17.4	20.0	19.5	22.8	16.9
Maryland	8.0	16.7	108.8	23.5	48.1	104.7	32.1	65.7	104.7
Pennsylvania	33.0	77.2	133.9	48.9	174.4	256.6	90.2	258.3	186.4
Virginia	12.8	35.7	178.9	15.0	52.8	252.0	29.4	90.6	308.2
West Virginia	13.4	17.8	32.8	12.7	39.3	209.4	26.8	58.2	117.2
Total	75.0	155.0	106.7	117.4	337.7	187.6	204.3	504.2	146.8
Region IV								
Alabama	95.4	97.6	2.3	19.3	72.2	274.1	117.2	172.9	47.5
Florida	66.8	103.2	54.5	27.1	108.7	301.1	96.4	215.8	123.9
Georgia	58.3	82.8	42.0	33.4	103.1	208.7	94.5	190.3	101.4
Kentucky	43.1	58.5	35.7	21.8	69.1	217.0	67.2	131.2	95.2
Mississippi	53.4	73.5	37.6	21.9	66.8	205.0	77.0	143.2	86.0
North Carolina	29.3	75.8	158.7	34.0	106.0	211.8	68.4	187.6	174.3
South Carolina	11.7	40.5	246.2	10.9	53.9	394.5	24.4	97.4	299.2
Tennessee	30.3	66.7	120.1	27.1	89.3	229.5	58.9	158.8	169.6
Total	388.3	598.6	54.2	195.5	669.1	242.3	604.0	1,297.2	114.8
Region V								
Illinois	26.7	44.6	67.0	112.9	156.0	38.2	141.8	203.4	43.4
Indiana	9.5	15.2	60.0	7.8	28.4	264.1	18.5	45.1	143.8
Michigan	33.0	55.5	68.2	70.9	129.2	82.2	106.2	187.7	76.7
Minnesota	9.9	14.7	48.5	16.5	25.1	52.1	27.4	40.8	48.9
Ohio	33.2	41.9	26.2	50.9	119.1	134.0	86.6	164.5	90.0
Wisconsin	26.1	38.3	46.7	13.9	55.3	297.8	40.9	95.3	133.0
Total	138.4	210.2	51.9	272.9	513.1	88.0	421.4	736.8	74.8

TABLE A-5—Continued

Region/State	Payments to Aged Recipients			Payments to Disabled Recipients			Total Payments to Aged, Blind, and Disabled Recipients		
	1973	1977[a]	Percent change	1973	1977[a]	Percent change	1973	1977[a]	Percent change
Region VI									
Arkansas	46.6	48.2	3.4	13.1	40.4	208.4	61.5	90.9	47.8
Louisiana	92.2	87.3	− 5.3	16.8	95.3	467.3	111.1	186.0	67.4
New Mexico	5.2	11.4	119.2	9.3	21.2	128.0	14.8	33.3	125.0
Oklahoma	42.3	61.3	44.9	26.8	52.9	97.4	70.5	116.1	64.7
Texas	114.1	160.3	40.5	26.4	130.3	393.6	144.2	296.5	105.6
Total	300.4	368.5	22.7	92.4	340.1	268.1	402.1	722.8	79.8
Region VII									
Iowa	9.5	11.0	15.8	3.6	15.5	330.6	14.4	28.1	95.1
Kansas	6.5	9.0	38.5	6.3	14.4	128.6	13.2	23.9	81.1
Missouri	89.6	64.7	−27.8	25.1	59.0	135.1	119.9	127.4	6.3
Nebraska	5.1	7.0	37.3	7.5	12.0	60.0	13.0	19.4	49.2
Total	110.7	91.7	−17.2	42.5	100.9	137.4	160.5	198.8	23.9
Region VIII									
Arizona	12.3	15.5	26.0	11.0	24.7	124.5	23.8	40.9	71.8
Colorado	24.3	26.1	7.4	13.8	31.4	127.5	38.4	58.1	51.3
Montana	1.9	2.5	31.6	3.4	6.7	97.1	5.5	9.4	70.9
North Dakota	4.2	3.7	−11.9	2.6	4.5	73.1	6.9	8.6	24.6
South Dakota	2.5	4.2	68.0	1.8	4.8	166.7	4.4	9.2	109.1
Utah	2.0	3.0	50.0	5.5	7.2	30.9	7.7	10.4	35.1

Wyoming	0.9	1.0	11.1	0.9	1.5	66.7	1.9	2.5	31.6
Total	48.1	56.0	16.4	39.0	80.8	107.2	88.6	139.1	57.0
Region IX									
California	386.9	538.0	39.1	379.0	850.7	124.5	793.7	1,432.1	80.4
Hawaii	4.0	7.1	77.5	4.5	8.0	77.8	8.7	15.4	77.0
Nevada	2.4	3.9	62.5	—c	3.2	—	2.5	7.8	212.0
Total	393.3	549.0	39.6	383.5	861.9	124.7	804.9	1,455.3	80.8
Region X									
Alaska	2.9	3.2	10.3	3.2	5.0	56.3	6.3	8.6	36.5
Idaho	2.6	3.7	42.3	3.8	7.6	100.0	6.5	11.5	76.9
Oregon	7.0	9.5	35.7	11.9	23.8	100.0	19.9	34.4	72.9
Washington	15.4	19.9	29.2	38.7	54.3	40.3	54.7	75.2	37.5
Total	27.9	36.3	30.1	57.6	90.7	57.5	87.4	129.7	48.4

NOTE: Detail may not add because of rounding.

a Partly estimated.

b Includes a total of more than $9 million not reported by states and paid to Indochinese refugees.

c No program.

SOURCES: *Social Security Bulletin, Annual Statistical Supplement, 1973*, table 145; and unpublished data provided by the Social Security Administration.